AFRI

Is There Hope?

Samuel M. Muriithi

University Press of America, Inc.
Lanham • New York • London

Copyright © 1996 by
University Press of America,® Inc.
4720 Boston Way
Lanham, Maryland 20706

3 Henrietta Street
London, WC2E 8LU England

Library of Congress Cataloging-in-Publication Data

Muriithi, Samuel M.
African crisis : is there hope? / Samuel M. Muriithi.
p.   cm.
Includes bibliographical references.
1. Africa--Economic conditions--1960- 2. Africa--Economic policy.
3. Africa--Population. 4. Africa--Colonial influence. 5. Democracy-
-Africa. 6. Management--Africa. I. Title.
HC800.M84   1996   338.96--dc20   95-51974 CIP

ISBN 0-7618-0245-2 (pbk: alk. ppr.)

DEDICATED TO
DOROTHY AND BILL ROSENBERGER
FOR YOUR LOVE AND CARE

TABLE OF CONTENTS

Preface

My goal of writing this book is to change the way Europeans, Americans, Asians and Africans view Africa and its crisis. Politicians and other decision makers, students, organizations, for example, World Bank and International Monetary Fund (IMF) have a pre-established notion of Africa. To others, Africa is a continent full of backward and lazy inhabitants. Others see Africa as a continent inhabited by sincere and honest persons; people of integrity and great wisdom. To others the continent is full of corrupt, arrogant, selfish and greedy people. The effect of these approaches is confusion, hatred, and lack of direction. Those who understand Africa are few and their decisions may not change the negative world-view and false theories. When there is civil war in Africa, the first reaction is to condemn the conflictors or invade the states. If famine occurs in Africa, the general reaction is, "Oh, those lazy chaps are on it again. They want food again." And any change in Europe or America is quickly introduced and dictated to Africa as a condition for political assistance. Imposed decisions are frequent and obvious.

Africans are to blame too. Often they accept decisions which are immature, irrelevant and illogical. Those who oppose certain practices are suppressed to make them quiet. When there is famine in one state, it is not uncommon to have government agencies confiscate "food aid" given and sell it for self-gain among its key personnel. Usually the world stands aside to watch Africa destroy itself. Most chaos in Africa only harm the Africans not outsiders. And crisis in Africa seems to have no end. Day after day, the crisis in Africa increases. Suffering of the weak -- women and children, refugees and small ethnic groups -- get worse. When peace comes to one village today, tomorrow the village is no more: all the occupants are killed with no particular reason given. Sorrow and grief continue. Living standards continue to decline as economies collapse and governments change hands. Africa is heading for the doom.

In this book, *African Crisis: Is There Hope?*, I'm confronting the question, "what hope is there in the midst of all the crisis in Africa?" Through research, case studies, personal experiences and contributions from my students, I have tried to give hope to the

hopeless. I have explored the causes of the current crisis from the social, political and economical point of view. It is my believe that
the book will challenge its readers to a point of action -- a point of reversing events in Africa in order to make the continent a better and safer place for all its people, irrespective of their ethnic social, religious or political background. The outsiders can assist change Africa, but the burden is on the Africans, to define the course of direction for the future. To survive, Africa must act now otherwise tomorrow might be too late. The book shows how to achieve this goal.

Acknowledgment

Writing a book is usually a hard task. It requires much time, effort and great contributions from many sources, individuals and authorities. It is through constructive criticisms and help that the final work of this edition was completed. As such, several people from both academic and non-academic professionals have played key roles to make the book a reality. It is impossible to mention all contributions and what they did or said. I'm thankful to all and your support. However, I owe a debt of gratitude to the following friends, colleagues and authorities. Of particular attention are:

Professors:

Dick Stallway, Department of Sociology, Northwest Nazarene College, Oregon.

Lisa Surdyk, School of Business and Economics, Seattle Pacific University, Seattle, Washington.

The above took the effort to read through the manuscript and offered their most profitable insights.

Editors:

Chris Ngui, former employee of World Vision International, Africa Region and Managing Director, Maarifa Limited.

Jane Ngui, Commerce Department, Daystar University, Nairobi, Kenya.

Pauline Kang'ethe, Seattle, Washington.

Thanks for your skills without which this work would be shapeless. Through your assistance, the book is able to convey its intended message.

Inspirers:

John Andor, Maritime Corporation, Seattle, Washington.

John Okoth Odera, Daystar University, Nairobi, Kenya.

Karen Flowers and Dick Flowers, Seattle, Washington.

Lisa, Pattye, John, Melissa, Natali, Pam, Jim and Chris, all of West 175 International, Seattle, Washington.

I greatly appreciates the time I spent with each one of you as you challenged me on different African issues. I hope this book answers your questions and concerns.

Thanks to my students for their continued contributions and desire to solve African crisis. The book should act as an eye opener to prepare you take charge in developing Africa.

Institutions:

Finally I'm grateful to the following institutions for allowing me to use their resources: The Computer Drome, Nairobi, Seattle Pacific University, Seattle Public Library, University of Washington Library, Daystar University, and West 175 International.

This is the fruits of your support. Thanks

Chapter One

Introduction

I write this book because, after teaching in Africa, my students and many African leaders have challenged me to write a book addressing African problems in a more realistic form. I agreed with my challengers that africa lacks books that address its problems using a practical approach. I have tried as much as possible to tackle issues that are important to the continent and which I believe can be a starting point to solving the ever increasing crisis in Africa.

Themes

There are four themes distinguished in this book. The first regards a critical analysis of the causes of the African crisis. The second is the effect of the crisis on the continent. The third is the available solutions. Finally, I have explored the future of the continent and its people. The themes set a trend and link events as they unfolded. My goal is to show how and what made Africa lag behind compared to other continents. I have also explored whether it is possible for Africa to rise to the level of the developed world's standard. Many books written on Africa have ignored a balanced approach to the past or current problems in Africa. Most books have blamed Africans or colonialists but have not gone beyond the blame. I have explored this issue further by balancing possible tactics that could ensure development in Africa. I believe development is a process, and Africa has to pass through the process, without which development is not possible.

Objectives

The objectives for this book are numerous:

The first objective is to show how Africans view the current crisis in their continent.

The second objective is to show how the Europeans and other outsiders explain the crisis in Africa.

The third objective is to show a critical analysis of the views presented by the groups.

The fourth objective is make sure that every chapter offers solutions to issues raised. I have used a question and answer approach to make the reader aware of the issue presented and participate in seeking solutions.

One major objective is to show that Africans are responsible for solving their own problems and the rest of the world can play a significant role in assisting the continent achieve this goal. The how this is done forms the backbone of the book.

Finally, I have used case studies where appropriate to reflect the real life situations in Africa. Most of the case studies come from research works written in Africa. Where Africans need to learn from the outside world, cases geared to that end are developed.

Book Audience

The primary audience of this book is university students and professors studying or teaching African development. The group is key in that it forms the future generation that can change the face of the continent. All universities in Africa, America, Europe and other parts of the world with a focus on Africa will benefit from the book, both as a text and a reference manual. This is a book that every student interested in African development needs in his or her library.

The Africa's leaders -- presidents, ministers, project managers, investors, politicians and the general public also are a target audience because they have direct involvement in the events in the continent. This group is responsible for the current affairs in Africa and will determine the future of the continent.

World decision makers from the World Bank, International Monetary Fund, and other financial leaders, all who determine the development trend of Africa form another target group. This group is responsible for measuring African development in comparison with the rest of the world.

Text Organization

There are ten chapters in all. The chapters are independent from each other, but a significant relationship exists, especially in chapters dealing with economic development of the continent. The goal is to make sure that each chapter explores critically its main objective. The chapters start with an introduction, which is followed by the chapter text. Finally, some chapters have case studies and questions that summarize the views presented in a practical way. The reader should answer the questions as a way of understanding the material presented.

Chapters' Organization

Chapter One: Introduction: This expresses the theme, objectives, goals, audience, and organization of the whole book.

Chapter Two: Colonialism: This chapter examines the role of colonial masters in Africa and how this has affected the continent. The major issue presented is whether the current events in Africa could be traced back to the colonialism era. The topic is relevant considering that there are major controversies today over whether colonizers are responsible for African problems.

Chapter Three: Democracy: This is a hot topic today. The world at large is advocating democracy for all nations as the only means of starting along the road to development. Africa, having been traditionally ruled by single parties for decades, found itself a victim of challenge. Most of the developed world nations have put strict measures in place that include freezing of donations to Africa in order to force the African governments to change their model of leaderships. This chapter examines whether democracy as advocated by other nations fits the African continent and its culture.

Chapter Four: Economy: This chapter traces back the economic trend as a model of development in Africa. Questions like whether the poor economic performance is related to past misuse of resources are addressed. All sectors of African development have been examined. A major focus is the role of Africa in the world economy.

Chapter Five: Management: The issue of African management of resources has been raised in many international meetings. Most of the world leaders have accused Africa leaders of being irresponsible and having misused all that is available for their own ends. Whether this accusation is true or false is the focus of the chapter. The chapter has also developed key strategies that must be followed in order to promote   effective management in African and other developing countries.

Chapter Six: Drought and Famine: The world is aware of the alarming death rates caused by starvation in Africa. Thousands upon thousands of people have died this way. The world has not been able to understand the reason behind this problem or why it is so severe only in Africa (the major focus for the world). This chapter looks at this problem in great depth. The goal is to make sure that the world understands the cause of drought and famine and how to work together with Africans to solve this epidemic.

Chapter Seven: Population: The world population is growing at a rate that will make it double by the year 2050. The 1994 Cairo Meeting on Population aimed at developing means necessary to control birth rates especially in developing countries. Africa, although the poorest continent, has the highest rate of birth in the world. It has been hard for the world to understand why a continent this poor should be unable to control its population. Resources in Africa have been unable to match the need for food and there is great fear that more and more people will continue to die of starvation in Africa. The chapter answers questions behind the high birth rates and why it is difficult to control. It also develops possible solutions that can aid Africa in curbing this problem.

Chapter Eight: Republic of South Africa: The chapter examines the Republic of South Africa since the coming of European and their influence in the country's economy, political structure and social life. The aim is go give a background to the complex relationship which has evolved over the years especially between the Whites minority and the Black majority.

Chapter Nine: The New South Africa: With the attainment of independence in South Africa for blacks, the question is how will all races work together after years of apartheid. The major focus is what freedom for the Blacks means to investors. I have also looked at different way which the new government aims at in order to improve living standards of the Blacks and create confidence among investors. Another issue addressed is the role the country can play in its effort to work with other countries in Africa to bring positive development of the continent.

Chapter Ten: Strategic Approach To African Crisis: The chapter gives a strategic approach to the problems presented in the book. It is a summary of the issues raised and how Africa can be developed. This is the most important chapter in this book as it gives solutions to the crisis in the continent.

Chapter Two

Colonialism: Is This The Root Of African Problems?

Once upon a time there was an old man who built his hut in the heart of the forest. He loved the forest and was friendly to all animals. As he walked in the forest, daily, he was happy to see the beauty of the land, and thanked God for it. He especially liked to listen to birds as they sang to their creator and wondered why he could not make such a joyous sound. One day, it started raining. The rain was too heavy that it made him to remain in the house for several days. Outside, the animals feared they might die. It was during this period that the elephant visited man and begged be allowed to warm its nose. The man pitied the forest giant and agreed to the request. Discovering the warmth was too nice, the elephant wanted to enter its whole body. The man feared his house would collapse and fall down, but the elephant insisted it would take care. In its effort to enter, the elephant forced its whole body into the hut, forcing the man outside. Seeing his generosity was abused, he set the house on fire. This made him to suffer greatly from the cold which eventually killed him.

The Europeans came to Africa like the elephant They tactfully urged for acceptance by the Africans. Later, they forced themselves into the African land, displacing the Africans. In resistance, many African men and women died in effort to rescue their land, a struggle which continued until independence.

When Europeans first came to Africa, they appeared friendly and respectful. People like John Kraft, John Rebman, Livingstone and Stanley came, either as explorers or missionaries. Their aim was either to open the continent to the White man's benefit or evangelize Africa. Hungry for the Good News, God's Message, many African societies accepted these men with much hospitality and concern. The Europeans received food, shelter, and protection. The missionaries in particular received favor from the communities served. Some are recalled for their great concern and love for Africans. However, following the missionaries were the traders, (missionary brothers as were they referred to by the Africans who did not distinguish the difference between different European groups). This group's interest was trade and getting raw material for industries in Europe. Finding Africa to be more rich in resources than previously thought, the traders asked their governments for protection from hostile Africans. Increases in the number of European traders led to increased competition. This resulted in a conflict of interest as to who was to control which part of Africa. Commenting on the European behavior, Burton O. Withhuhn in his article entitled The Impress of Colonialism has noted: "As the number of European states operating in Africa increased, the competition between them grew, and each found it desirable to operate from specific territorial bases" (Knight et el. 1976:31). The European behavioral change shocked many Africans who failed to understand why the Europeans behaved strangely.

To avoid conflict as different European groups settled in Africa, Bismarck, the ruler of Germany conferred a meeting in Berlin in 1884. The meeting decided how to partition Africa between the European powers and established rules to control conflict of interest, fear, and economic ambitions. It was this meeting that set the ground work for the scramble of Africa. The result was Europeans' settlement in Africa as no man's land. Africa's partition was like a piece of chicken or pie among the Europeans whose interests ignored the interests of Africans who had lived on the land for generations. Africans became secondary tools requiring little or no consideration. By 1900 over 90 percent of the African continent had fallen under European occupation and control. Boundaries to denote nation groups and the areas they occupied took effect. The French and British took West Africa, and the British and Germany took East Africa -- later the Germans left Tanganyika during World War 1, leaving the British in control. The Portuguese took Angola and Mozambique while the Dutch had already established themselves in Southern Africa since 1652. The Italians' effort to control Ethiopia was a failure. They suffered defeat and were forced to leave the country. In 1879, a substantial part of Africa was under European control with France in Algeria and Senegal, Britain along the Gold Coast and at the Cape, and Portugal in Angola and Mozambique. By 1914 the entire African continent was under European control except for Ethiopia and Liberia. The table below shows different Europeans' settlements in Africa:

Table 2.1

Political Divisions in Africa in 1914	Square Miles
France (Tunisia, Algeria, Morocco, French West Africa, French Congo, French Somalia land, Madagascar)	4,086,950
British (Union of South Africa, Basutoland, Bechuanaland, Nyasaland, Rhodesia, British East Africa, Uganda, Zanzibar, Somali land, Nigeria, Gold Coast, Sierra Leone, Gambia,	3,704,311
German (East Africa, South-West Africa, Cameroon, Togo-land)	910,150
Belgium (Congo State)	900,000
Portuguese (Guinea, West Africa, East Africa)	787,500
Italian (Eritrea, Italian Somali land, Libya)	600,000
Spanish (Rio de Oro, Muni River Settlements)	79,800
Independent States (Liberia, Ethiopia)	393,000
TOTAL	11,458,811

(L. S. Stavrianos in his publication THE WORLD SINCE 1500: A Global History, 2/e, c11971, 390. Reprinted by permission of Prentice-Hall, Upper Saddle River, New Jersey.

AFRICAN RESPONSE

Africans are faithful to promises, covenants and agreements. When the Europeans started to settle in Africa, the Africans were not surprised or worried. They did not resist when requested for treaties to administer boundaries. According to them, the Europeans appeared promising and faithful. The Africans trusted the promises that the foreign powers made.

The African leadership did not interfere with the land that belonged to both the living and the dead. The Europeans took advantage of the african sincerity, and lack of education. Through manipulation of the African minds and illiteracy level, the Europeans made them sign over their rights to their land. The Europeans felt a great desire to settle in Africa and did all they could to achieve this goal. This made them give little thought to the African culture or the way of life. In his observation Burton Withhuhn has noted that:

> . . . . It is increasingly clear that the explorers and early colonialists frequently took inappropriate actions because they did not understand the implications of what they were observing. Land standing idle was assumed unused. Weakly defined territorial bounders were considered evidence of poorly articulated political systems. Spatially separated political areas were clearly a sign of backwardness. These and other incorrect judgments made the external impress of alien impact all the more burdensome to the peoples affected. It is not surprising, that the modifications and reorganizations, or the society, forced by the contract, promoted the emergence of new African territorial states (Knight et el. 1976: p. 38).

The effects of the Berlin treaty were far reaching. The treaty required effective occupation of territories claimed by the European states. Different European powers used varied approaches to win Africans and to ensure that the intended territories came under the control of the new masters. In most cases, force was inevitable, although some areas required only small forces. For example, in West Africa, Colonial Kembell overran Sokotra with only twelve hundred men. The British attack against Ijebu-Ode consisted of a thousand men while General Dobbs successfully led two thousand men against Dahomey with an army of twelve thousand men. There are several reasons associated with European success. These include the following:

1. There was a dissension among Africans that prevented them from uniting against a common enemy. This gave the Europeans a chance to organize African communities against each other.

2. Some African leaders cooperated with Europeans against historical traditional enemies. For example, in West Africa, the Ahmadu of Segou joined the French to fight Mahmadou Lemine. Similarly, Tieba of Sikasso conspired against Samori while Ibadan joined the British to defeat Ijebu.

3. Outcasts received training to enable them to participate in the army. These people had been expelled from the communities as they were considered to be useless. As such, they were completely dependent on the foreigners who fed them, clothed them, trained them and paid them. Most of these people participated in fighting other tribes using European tactics and direction.

4. Divide-and-rule: The British Government used the divide and rule method. The administration organized, for example, the men in the Northern Nigeria Regiment on the basis of language groups and used them separately as they desired.

5. Poor fighting techniques: Another reason why Africans suffered defeat easily was their inability to change their battle techniques to match the enemies. Many of them persisted in waging frontal, head-on warfare, a method that left them like ducks to the murderous firepower. After defeat, the Africans retreated to their walled cities, where they were vulnerable to European artillery.

6. Aggressiveness and ruthlessness of the European officers who did not want to appear weak in the eyes of their mother governments. They were sure of earning promotion and popularity by occupying as much land as possible. Also, they were sure of support from their mother governments. Take for example, Lord Laggard saw great rationalization after the destruction in Munshi towns and villages in Nigeria during the 1900 expedition. He notes:

> I cannot but express my sense of regret at the very great loss of life among these ignorant savages, and the burning of the villages with their food. The Munshis however are most intractable people, and nothing except extremely severe chastisement of this sort will prevent them from lawless murders and looting of canoes, or induce them to allow the telegraph to be constructed through their country. My own view is that it is far more humane, in the event, to inflict a drastic lesson at first and thoroughly subdue people of this kind than to attempt half measures, which invariably lead to a further outbreak and a greater eventual loss of life (Cited by S. C. Ukpabi, " British Colonial Wars in West Africa: Image and Reality, " Civilizations XX (1970): 396.

Where the Europeans and the Africans' world views conflicted, it was hard to gain a common understanding, and probably has never been achieved. It was when the European powers started to put various groups together and used power to rule them that many Africans started to realize their mistakes. They saw the Europeans as insincere and having failed their part of the promises. Reacting to this behavior in 1911, a Nyasaland African wrote this scathing criticism of the hypocrisy of European Christians:

There is too much failure among all Europeans in Nyasaland. The three combined bodies --- Missionaries, Government and Companies or gainers of money --- do form the same rule to look upon the native with mockery eyes. It sometimes startles us to see that the three combined bodies are from Europe, and along with them there is a title Christendom. And to compare and make a comparison between the Master of the title and his servants, it provokes any African way from believing in the Master of the title. If we have power enough to communicate ourselves to Europe, we would advise them not to call themselves Christendom, but Europeandom. Therefore the life of the three combined bodies are altogether too cheaty, too thefty, too mockery. Instead of "Give," they say "Take away from." There is too much breakage of God's pure law as seen in James's Epistle, Chapter five, verse four. (Cited by R. Oliver and A. Atmore 1967: 158).

Discovering that the Europeans had cheated and taken advantage of their ignorance, the Africans were very bitter. This led African tribesmen to come together with a common goal: "To get ride of the common enemy." This led to the struggle for independence all over Africa. The struggle continued until the 1960s and 1970s when a majority of the countries gained independence.

THE COLONIAL IMPACT IN AFRICA

Both directly and indirectly, colonialism bears much blame for the current and future crisis in Africa. Africa was a combination of deeply cultured societies. They followed specific procedures in order to maintain a standard life. The Africans knew how to balance their economic, social and political needs to avoid misuse of resources. All resources -- land and people belonged to God. Each person in the community was responsible for the management of resources.
Generation after generation came and went, yet life was the same and

none complained. Tribal wars came and went and people were happy when they won and became victorious. If defeated, they did not give up and worked hard to win next time. Both men and women passed through traditional rituals that made them "true" men and women in the eyes of the society. It was a source of pride to pass through societal rituals. Those who opposed the practices became outcasts and were either killed or expelled from the societies. Medicine men, farmers, blacksmiths, headers and worriers found their roles in the societies. The society recognized each man's role. Age differences gave seniority much authority and respect between the old and the young.

The coming of Europeans meant a total change of the whole traditional settings. The societies changed from both within and without. The politics, social life, economy, and religion of the people came under direct influence of Western ideologies. Let us consider how this happened.

POLITICAL IMPACT

The African societies were politically different and each community had its own way of managing affairs. While some had kings, others had none. For example, Kabakas of Uganda ruled the Bagandas community as king. This was a certain kingship lineage. In West Africa, several chiefdoms existed --- Dahomey, Mali, Asante and Ashante are good examples. In South Africa, Shaka the Zulu was the Chief and King of the Zulu. Mirambo was a King of the Nyamwenzi of Central Tanganyika. In Kenya, Chief Kivoi was a known Chief of the Kamba community while Laibons were the Masaai leaders. Communities without chiefs or kings, for example, the Kikuyu of Central Kenya, had elders as rulers.

Upon the coming of the Europeans, however, they imposed their own style of leadership in Africa. Africans were to submit to the new leadership or be punished. They were subject to authoritarian and dictatorial leadership that replaced mutual understanding and consultation. The latter had existed for generations. The Europeans administered boundaries wherever they felt appropriate. Such boundaries often divided the same community as if they were enemies. Hostile tribes that were enemies for centuries became neighbors. This led to conflicts that exist to the present. Several examples are evident. In Kenya and Tanzania's border, the Masaai community found itself divided by a border, leading to two groups of Masaai. This has caused great problems of cattle stealing. If Kenyan Masaai close the border and steal cows from their neighbors in Tanzania, the chase stops upon entering Kenya, and vice versa. The Masaai community in the area has not recognized border existence and continues to cause problems. As a result, there is a frequent crisis between the two groups and the two governments have to keep monitoring the situation. Kenya and Uganda's border divide the Luos who belonged to the same group. In case there is a problem between the two countries, the groups support each other as they see themselves as brothers and sisters. A similar problem exists along the Kenya and Somali border. The Somali communities are on either side of the border, and it is hard to tell which group belongs to either country. Likewise, Rwanda and Uganda have experienced the same crisis along their borders. In South Africa, tribes like the Zulu, the Xhosa and the Ngoni appear widely spread in South African Republic, Zimbabwe, and Zambia, making it difficult to monitor movements.

Many guerrilla movements in Africa are blamed on a neighboring country, as place of organizations and coordination. Countries such as Burundi and Rwanda have experienced tribal upheavals as different groups have used parts of the country to prepare attacks on their governments. The 1994 brutal murdering of the hundreds of innocent people has its roots in the colonial era when rival groups where placed together. Many civil wars are caused as a result of a country allowing opposition groups to operate activities meant to undermine neighboring governments. As a result, governments frequently accuse each other of interfering with internal affairs. Whether this is true or not, the blame goes back to the colonizers who set boundaries without considering ethnic differences.

In order for the Europeans to have significant effects in Africa, they made sure that African authorities were either displaced or suppressed. While some collaborated with the new administration, others became victims of manipulation before they could realize the motives of the foreigners. Others suffered great losses of human life as many of them were killed. Worse still are those Africans who served as spies for their masters. They became agents of attacking and spying on their neighbors who remained stubborn. Different foreign groups used the Kabakas of Uganda to their advantages over each other. The groups included different missionary groups, Protestants, Catholics and Muslims. This led to Kabakas' failure to take concrete action or realize what was happening. During the struggle between the groups, the one favored by the Kabakas led to the persecution of the opposing groups. It was during the process of such struggles that all different missionary groups came together and defeated him and placed their choice. In West Africa, the Asante victimized smaller tribes in to submission to the British rule.

The European approach to African political structures meant a change of African political systems. Individual destinies and environmental controls were impossible. Land that was considered to be communal was put under foreign control. Its control was strict and punishable.

Being powerless, the Africans abandoned their ancestral land and squeezed into small lands that were less productive. They had to make room for settlers who started big plantations growing coffee, tea, cocoa, sisal, and sugarcane. It was in the plantations that Africans became laborers. The best land went to the settlers and Africans became squatters. In some cases, they settled on the marginal areas that could not support them and made them more dependent on their masters. Settled in villages, they had only small pieces of land, if any, where they grew onions and flowers as dictated by the colonizers. For example, in Kenya, the cool highlands on the Abadares and Mau ranges became the White Highlands and Africans were settled small pieces of land as assigned. The Rift Valley was used for growing wheat or for ranches for keeping thousands of cows and sheep. In South Africa, Zambia, Zimbabwe and Angola, the Africans suffered the same fate as they became slaves in their own land. They suffered but "without bitterness" to avoid punishment.

ECONOMIC IMPACT

Economically, Africa suffered through a transformation from a productive continent to total ruins. Before the colonizers' arrival, Africans had their own system of trade, barter trade. The communities knew what each other demanded and aimed at satisfying those needs. For example, while pastoral societies had much wealth of cows and sheep and goats, they had little or no food. Similarly, the agricultural community had much food, like millet and cassava. To satisfy their needs, the two groups exchanged what each desired. Black-smiths also traded by providing the communities with spears, knives, hoes and other iron tools. They also received whatever they required. A community like the Ndorobo of East Africa lived in the forest and harvested honey that they provided to the Kikuyu, Kamba, Masaai, Luhyia, either for brewing bear or as food substitutes while in turn they received milk, meat, millet and sorghum.

Tran-Sahel trade also existed across Africa. Arabs from North Africa brought salts and other merchandise to the South and received palm oil, cocanuts, cocoa, gold, and yams from West and Central

Africa. For a long time, the Arabs also traded with East African people.

In all these trades, there were medium traders who acted like today's salesmen and retailers. They knew who needed what and where to get it. The people liked their economic environments that reflected their needs and preferences.

To satisfy their desires, the colonizers systematically designed and exploited the African resources to meet their needs. Resource evaluation was on the basis of what they could produce in Europe. By channeling raw material to Europe, this led to a dependence that exists to date. African sources of income and later foreign currency were subject to European measurement and satisfaction. The continent became the source of raw material like minerals, cash crops, and cheap labor. Big plantations of coffee, tea, cocoanut, rubber, pyrethrum, sisal and cotton led to removal of dense natural vegetations. To some communities, this was dehumanizing the "mother land" that provided for the people. The African small industries like pottery and weaving gave way to imports from Europe.

The goal of the European powers was to promote export meant for colonial economies that would provide needed raw materials in Europe. British officials for instance assumed that it was the duty of the colonies to import British manufactured goods. By 1922, about twenty-six governments had done so although not entirely on their own free will. This "imperial reference" proved a godsend to the hard pressed British industries in the 1930s during the depression period. Sir Philip Conliffer-Lister of Colonial office noted this in April 1932 in the Common:

> I am not sure that it is realized enough what a standby that Colonial trade has been in the difficult years. . . . In 1924 only 6.8% of our export trade was done with the colonial empire. In 1931 that proportion has risen to over 10%, and that at a time when values were crashing in the Colonies and their purchasing power has been enormously diminished. That shows the value of that trade, and it emphasizes. . . . how very wide and valuable were the preferences which had for years past been given by those Colonies to this country. Since this House took its decision [on imperial preference] in February new preferences have been given. . . . The result is that nearly every colony that has a tariff on manufactures and which is free to do it at the moment is giving a substantial preference on this country (Breff 1973:150).

A major and serious exploitation of human resources was the misuse of Africa's beautiful natural resources in order to satisfy the needs of foreign markets. In West Africa, for instance, French assumed that Senegal could best produce the groundnut cash crops and directed agronomic research and infrastructure overlooking the fact that the country's being suitable for other agricultural products like cattle raring, rice, and sugar cane cultivation, fruits, early vegetables and palm oil. Senegal would have benefited more if the capital spent on behalf of one crop was allocated to the comprehensive development of other crops and natural resources in general. This way, the country would be in a better position today.

Colonizers' self-gratification became obviously demonstrated by the way they treated African natural resources. They made sure that industries did not take priority and efforts for promotions were frustrated. In East Africa, for example, it was feasible to manufacture simple products of mass consumption such as cotton textiles, shoes, furniture, and matches. Similarly, processing was done on local materials into semi-manufactured state before exporting. If the whole process was done in Africa, this would have provided jobs and skills for the Africans. Unfortunately, efforts to establish industries in Africa faced opponents as such moves were unproductive to the colonies. This became obvious at the 1935 Governor Conference, which considered a proposal to establish a blanket factory in Uganda. The governor of the colony opposed the project saying that "if industries undertakings were started in East Africa, a certain loss of revenue through the falling off of customs duties might accrue to Uganda." A similar opposition was aired by the governor of Tanganyika who justified his position by quoting from a dispatch from the Secretary of State (Dec. 4, 1935). " . . . that it was undesirable to accelerate the industrialization of East Africa which must, for many years to come, remain a country of primary produce (Breff, 1973:274)." With many Europeans having the same views, Africa was only good as a source of raw material for Europe.

By the time European left Africa, much destruction had been done to the environment. It is this destruction which has led to desert expansion in most of Africa today. Convinced that their small industries were useless and inferior, the African felt discouraged and abandoned them. Africa as a continent became unimportant and uninteresting. Climate changes started to occur due to cutting of forests, mines, leading to deep channels, holes and many useless landscape. Africans became slaves who received low wages or sometimes nothing but maize flour, enough to sustain life. With the development of industries in the urban areas and mine centers, migration from rural to urban areas began, a process evident even today. This migration affected males who traditionally were the sole bread winners. The effect was that many African women and children were left in the country side. The city, being far, caused men to spend much money on transportation and they had little if any to improve their families.

SOCIAL IMPACT

As already noted, the political and economic stability of Africa suffered upon the Europeans' settlement. The coming of Europeans to Africa meant a transfer of their culture to Africa. The Europeans termed African traditional beliefs as evil and greatly condemned the practices. The traditional rituals like circumcision, sacrificial offering, beating drums and dancing were denounced. The Western style of worship replaced different African traditional religious practices. To those who objected to such practices, they became victims of shame to their societies. The church expelled or excommunicated these victims from participating in all activities. In response, the Africans formed their own churches. They were churches that performed all activities in the European churches but also allowed some traditional practices like polygamy, beating of drums, and circumcision.

On the family systems, the European settlers introduced monogamy as the ideal marriage for the whole human race. The practice was derived from the Jewish Bible's teachings, something which the Africans found difficult to comprehend. To the Africans, this was a new concept. Not that some African men did not have only one wife, but it was never a rule as meant by Europeans. Husbands with more wives were either to divorce them or be expelled from the church. Some submitted to divorcing rather than being eternally condemned. The majority retained their wives and family structure, a structure that is only changing due to economic hardship in many African countries.

An African man felt proud when identified as a husband of many wives and a father of many children. He knew he had a name when he died because his lineage would continue. Among the Kikuyu, the Luhyia, and the Luos of Kenya, a man of one wife was useless and could not address a group of elders. His fame depended on the number of wives he could command. Traditionally, boys and girls were treated differently. While boys were expected to be independent, brave and courageous, girls were expected to be humble and submissive. The difference was distinct as the two sexes matured. The man took control of the society while the wife took her position in the kitchen.

The coming of Europeans to Africa meant a different life style. They considered all African beliefs and practices to be evil. To them, the practices needed to be replaced. This led to the introduction of the European ways of life as the classic life in Africa that all communities were to copy. The Portuguese ensured all African names were changed to Portuguese names while the French assimilated their colony with their way of life.

In an effort to do away with this practice, President Mobutu Sese Seko of Zaire promoted African style of dressing among his people upon becoming the president. In the same way, Mwalimu Julius Nyerere of Tanzania encouraged his people to use Swahili as a medium of communication instead of English or tribal languages. Political leaders in Africa also rose up against the Europeans. Among them were Mzee Jomo Kenyatta, Kenya, Kwame Nkrumah, Ghana, Julius Nyerere, Tanzania, Dr. Kenneth Kaunda, Zambia, and Dr. Sam Nunjoma, Namibia. These men played major roles in pioneering independence struggles and in the final independence of their countries. The leaders under their organized party started struggle against Europeans that saw many countries claim independence by the dawn of the 1960s.

Upon independence, however, European colonizers abandoned the continent. They left much confusion, and little development. They had only improved areas that benefited them and many areas remained unknown to development. There were roads and railways but little education for leaders. The educated few were to bring their countries out of confusion. They were the saviors and heroes.

With resources destroyed, cultures ruined, and political systems changed, the leaders did not know which directions to take. The Europeans in turn offered assistance. They offered development funds, expatriates, materials and technical help to the countries. As a result, the past economical and political distortions persisted and led to total dependence on the Western nations.

The plantations' produce and minerals continued to be key exports to Europe. These have remained the sources of foreign exchange and government revenues. This approach did not benefit Africa in any way. With the long term price falling due to competition in agricultural products, as compared to manufactured goods from Europe, African governments could not afford to cover debts. As a result, there were cuts in imports and budgetary restraints in Africa countries. It is a situation they have not yet recovered from. The Europeans took no effort to restore African resources to a state of positive development. Further discussion of this topic is in Chapter Four.

CASE STUDY 2.1

THE MODEL OF "ORIGINAL SIN": RISE OF THE WEST AND LAG OF THE REST

THIS CASE WAS PREPARED BY PROFESSOR WILLIAM DARITY. JR. OF DEPARTMENT OF ECONOMICS, UNIVERSITY OF NORTH CAROLINA AT CHAPEL HILL. IT WAS A PAPER PREPARED AND PRESENTED AT THE ASSA SESSION. LANCE DAVIS OFFERED CONSTRUCTIVE CRITICISM TO THE PAPER WHILE ALAN KYLE WINDAHAM SHARED HIS SURVEY OF HISTORICAL RESEARCH ON THE BRITISH EXPORT TRADE OF FIREARMS TO AFRICA BETWEEN THE 17TH AND 19TH CENTURIES.

The close temporal association between slave trading and colonial slavery in the Americas and the emergence of an industrial Europe from the 16th through 19th centuries has suggested a cause-effect relationship to some scholars. Most notable among these is Eric Williams (1966) who proposed that for Britain, in particular, the colonial slave system was instrumental in achieving successful capitalist economic development. Indeed, Williams's study suggests the hypothesis that the slave trade lies at the heart of the origins of the disparity in economic status between Europe and Africa. The hypothesis has been given full development in Walter Rodney's (1972) provocatively-titled book, *How Europe Underdeveloped Africa.*

While economic historians whose research interests have been devoted to explaining European industrialization typically have ignored Williams's analysis (Darity, 1990 pp. 118-20). When they have considered his claims their conclusions have registered on the negative side of the ledger. Their basis for dismissal of Williams's arguments that modern European prosperity derives from exploitation of coerced African labor in the Americas has been empirical. Stanley L. Engerman (1972) and Patrick K. O'Brien (1982) put forth the "small ratios" argument to undercut Williams (i.e., slave trade profits, colonial trade, and export activity constituted such small shares of British or European gross national products or gross investment that they are irrelevant in explaining the rise of industry). On the other hand, the other prong of the Williams-Rodney hypothesis, the adverse long-term effect of the slave trade on African economic development has garnered virtually no attention from mainstream economic historians.

Several responses have been made to the "small ratios" argument, including those in papers by Barbara Solow (1985), Ronald W. Bailey (1986), Ronald Findlay (1990), and myself (Darity, 1990). These responses point out that, from a historical perspective, the proportions computed by Engerman and by O'Brien actually are quite large. While they might appear to be "small" in absolute size, when compared with similar figures for various countries at various times, their relative magnitudes are quite substantial. However, such numbers are not decisive. For the ratios to be vested with interpretative substance they must be integrated into a theoretical framework that would indicate their potential significance.

O'Brien and Engerman apparently now concede both points handsomely. In their recent collaborative paper (1991 p. 178) they issue the welcome acknowledgment that "expressing the value of the output produced within any sector of economic activity as a percentage of national income seems almost calculated to create an impression of insignificance." They then proceed to report trade statistics that indicate a major role for colonial trade for England in the 18th century, although they remain agnostic about the importance of colonial trade in the 17th century.

They then go on to admit that the significance of the export sector only can be established in the context of a theoretical model. Virtually echoing a portion of my discussion (Darity, 1990 pp. 122-3, 126, 128). O'Brien and Engerman (1991 p. 187) observe that "The significance of exports is derogated by using national income as the sole point of reference. Foreign trade needs to be considered in the context of a dynamic general equilibrium model that considers the contribution of exports (and other sources of changes in demand) to the cycles of growth achieved by the British economy from 1697 to 1802."

Three major extant formal models of slavery and the slave plantation system now exist in which foreign trade can be given the context that O'Brien and Engerman (1991) now say is required. These are models developed by Solow (1985), Darity (1982a), and Findlay (1990). Each of these models has its limitations.

Solow's model is quasi-Ricardian (see David Ricardo, 1951), featuring two regions, Europe and the Colonies. Neither Africa nor the slave trade is modeled explicitly. European production is characterized by increasing returns. The cheaper production opportunities afforded by the colonial region, which depends upon African slave labor, prop up the general rate of profit available to European capitalists and sustain a higher rate of growth for Europe than would prevail otherwise.

While Solow says that her model is evocative of Eric Williams's theory of British industrialization, the textual basis for her claim is not obvious. Certainly Williams's (1966 pp. 113, 145, 150-1) consistent invocation of the "old law of slave production" -- the propensity for cultivation by slave labor to exhaust soil -- is incompatible with the view that there were increasing returns in plantation agriculture.

Solow's technological asymmetry between Europe and the colonies seems to owe more to a brief but pregnant comment from Richard Sheridan (1973 pp. 15-16): "As artificial creations tied to the metropolis by the Acts of Trade, the export economies in the West Indies came to play a significant role in the economic development of Great Britain. Essentially the growth process involved the diversion of capital and labor from domestic agriculture and conspicuous consumption, activities subject to the law of decreasing returns, into Atlantic empire trade and manufacturing for export, activities which came to yield increasing returns." Even here, the increasing returns activities are "Atlantic empire trade and manufacturing for export," not slave-grown sugar or tobacco in the colonies.

If the Solow model were to capture an authentically Ricardian story, colonial produce would have to have been a staple component of the European workers' consumption bundle. It also would have to have been produced cheaply enough in the colonies to reduce Europe's labor costs to bolster the rate of profit: this need not require an assumption of increasing returns. While the latter conditions appear to have been met, Sidney Mintz's (1985 pp. 46, 115, 173-7) study suggests that in the case of England, at least, sugar was not viewed as an essential element of working-class diets until the 19th century, a bit late in the game.

The formal models advanced by Darity (1982a) and Findlay (1990) both are variants of neoclassical general equilibrium trade models. Both treat all three regions of the triangle forming the Atlantic economy in a highly aggregated fashion. Unlike Findlay's version, my model neglects to distinguish between stocks and flows of slaves in the Americas. It also lacks an explicit representation of the process for the production of slaves for the export trade on the African continent and fails to treat the export of European manufacturers to Africa, to be exchanged for slaves, as part of the structure of trade.

Findlay's model corrects the foregoing shortcomings of my model. However, it shares an additional weakness with my model. The neoclassical trade framework is not readily amenable to displaying the phenomenon of special interest with respect to Europe: structural transformation. Findlay (1990 p.11) is left treating the Industrial Revolution"as [an exogenous] Hicks-neutral shift in the production function " for Europe's manufacturing sector, when the thrust of Eric

Williams's analysis indicates that the Industrial Revolutions was an endogenous outcome of the repercussions of the slave system in the Americas.

An alternative and more natural route for modeling the Williams-Rodney hypothesis can be found via a Keynesian approach. Here the emphasis shifts to differential multiplier effects associated with various sectors of the economy because of variations in backward and forward intersector linkages (Albert O.Hirshman, 1958). The colonial trade sector, inclusive of the slave trade and slave-grown produce, displayed a remarkable and unique array of intersectoral linkages of both types for Europe and especially for Britain. Hence the multiplier effects were bound to be quite substantial. If, correspondingly, the consequence of participation in the slave trade was to retard such multipliers effects in Africa, a disparity could rise between "the West" and "the Rest" ("the West" is not merely a spatial concept, since Africa is no less in the West geographically than Europe).

In Chapter 23 of his General Theory, John Maynard Keynes (1936 pp. 333-51) asserted that his vision of aggregate demand-led growth bore a strong resemblance to the views of them much-maligned mercantilists who "were under no illusions as to the nationalistic character of their policies and their tendency to promote war. It was national advantage and relative strength at which they were admittedly aiming" (p.348). Although Keynes did not share the mercantilists' desire to repress domestic wages, which would make export capacity even more important as a source of aggregate demand, it should not be surprising that some of the mercantilist writers should sound like early Keynesians. For example, the 17th century mercantilist Josiah Child (p.205) estimated that each white planter engaged in sugar cultivation in the islands utilizing black slaves generated an employment multiplier effect of four additional English jobs because of the planter's demand for clothing, household goods, and the like.

Sir Thomas Dalby (1972 p. 27) expressed a related sentiment in 1690 when making his case for elimination of the Royal African Company's monopoly position in the trade. Dalby estimated that the value of the iron products used as work tools by the 600,000 slaves then in the West Indies amounted to 200,000 pounds sterling. He concluded, " . . . the produce and Consumption with the Shipping they give Employment to, is of an Infinite deal more benefit to the Wealth, Honor, and Strength of the Nation, than four times the same Number of Hands the best Employed at Home can be."

Were these mercantilist writers engaged in mere hyperbole with their speculative estimate of the multiplier effects of the slave system? No. The direct effects of the slave trade were profound, raising villages like Liverpool in England and Nantes and Bordeaux in France to the status of cities. Those Europeans who profited from slavery sometimes amassed great fortunes which they transferred to industrial employment and to the insurance and banking sectors (e.g., the cases of Lloyd's and Barclays' Bank [Williams, 1966 pp. 98-105, 126-34). What was not transferred was often expended in conspicuous consumption, further augmentating the stream of aggregate demand: witness Williams's (pp. 85-920 description of the lifestyles of the absentee West Indian landlords in England.

The range of backward linkages from the slave trade and slave plantation system was extensive. The development of the cotton textile industry in 18th-century England, so closely identified with the Industrial Revolution, was fueled by the export trade that provided fabrics to purchase slaves on the African coast and clothing for the slaves on the plantations (Joseph E. Inikori, 1989). In the 17th century, English manufacturers already were shipping brass, amber, blankets, bells, beads, cloth, carpets, pistols, gunpowder, silk, hats, knives, beef, bread, butter, sugar, medicines, and liquor to Africa to be exchanged for African produce. However, it was woolen textiles that came heavily into play in the trade of slaves (Wilson E. Williams, 1938 p.9).

Manchester was the first great manufacturing center in England. Its growth was linked intimately to Liverpool slavers' requirements for exports to Africa to obtain slaves. Wilson Williams (1938 p. 14) in a thesis that influenced Eric Williams, wrote, "Since Liverpool made Manchester, the connection of Africa with the evolution of capitalism in England is thus rendered very clear." To the extent that Manchester made not only cotton textiles for export to the slave coast and to the plantations but also imported raw cotton from the Americas, it received what Eric Williams (1966 p. 71) called a "double stimulus." Moreover, the West Indies generally served as an important outlet for English manufacturers. Dalby was alert to the significance of the West India Market for English iron mongers, the latter producing not only tools for plantation agriculture but also the chains of the African trade; furniture and pottery makers also benefited (W. Williams, 1938 p. 39).

Bristol, the second largest British slave port, was the site of a major shipbuilding industry whose development also depended upon the trade to Africa (W. Williams, 1938 pp. 11-13). Even Birmingham's growth can be joined closely to the slave-trade, for among the array of goods shipped to Africa to be traded for slaves were Birmingham firearms. Limited   evidence suggests that guns and gunpowder constituted 10-30 percent of the value of cargoes exchanged for slaves

(R. A. Kea 1971: George Metcalf, 1987). Anywhere from 1.6 to 1.9 million firearms were shipped to West Africa in the interval 1776-1805. This aspect of the trade gave rise to the notorious slave-gun cycle: slaves were exchanged for firearms that were used to procure more slaves to be traded for more guns, and so on (Inikori, 1977: Herbert Foster, 1976).

The major forward linkage from the slave trade and slave plantation system was the sugar output of the West Indies. As Findlay (1990 p. 22) points out, it is important to recognize that what Britain imported was raw, unrefined sugar, syrup, or molasses; therefore, "In good Mercantilist fashion, the final processing into refined white sugar and the distillation of molasses into rum were reserved for the industry of the mother country. . . . Differentiated tariffs provided the necessary 'effective protection' for hundreds of sugar-refining establishments in Bristol, Glasgow, and London, which was the main center." Glasgow also imported raw tobacco to be processed into smoking materials for consumers (E. Williams, 1966, p. 75).

Karl Marx's incandescent rhetoric did not miss the mark:

> The colonial system ripened trade and navigation as in a hothouse. . . . The colonies provided a market for the budding manufactures, and a vast increase in accumulation which was guaranteed by the mother country's monopoly of the market. The treasures captured outside Europe by undisguised looting, enslavement and murder flowed back to the mother-country and were turned into capital there (1977 p. 918).

But what of Africa? There, Marx's "hothouse" effect was altogether absence. The most lucrative activity throughout the 18th century for those Africans with the power to enslave rather than be enslaved was procurement of human exports for the slave trade. As Walter Rodney (1972 p. 115) observed: " . . . even the busiest African in West, Central or East Africa was concerned more with trade than with production, because of the nature of the contacts with Europe: and that situation was not conducive to the introduction of technological improvement because their role and preoccupation [with the slave trade] took their minds and energies away from production." The wealth of the African elite was bound to exchange activity, leading them to send abroad the essential source of wealth in production: labor (Darity, 1982b, pp. 13-15).

Inikori (1986 p. 3) emphasizes the adverse effects of depopulation, resulting from the export slave trade, on the extent of the African market. The salutary effects Adam Smith forecast for a region anticipating growth in markets were inverted: " . . . between 1450 and 1879, export demand for captives kept the total population of tropical Africa at a level that was far too low to stimulate as widespread development of the division of labor, the growth of internal trade, diversification of the economy, transformation of the technology and organization of production, and class differential. At the same time export demand for captives retarded the development of commodity production for export . . . "

The African failure to pursue mercantilist principles, while the Europeans were doing exactly that in mobilizing slave-based economics in the Americas, began the process of uneven development. Inikori (1982 p.55) knows of "no historical example of an economy in which the technology and organization of industrial production were transformed during a period of uncontrolled importation of cheap foreign manufactures."

Africa lost, in Inikori's (1982 p. 54) estimation, 300 years of economic development. Heavy involvement in the export slave trade deprived it of a general industrial stimulus. Here was the incubus for comparative African economic backwardness, reinforced during the period of external colonial rule that followed the end of the slave trade (Inikori, 1982 p. 54). Here was the "original sin" that began the partition between the rich and poor regions.

Source: William Darity, Jr. *The Model of Original Sin: Rise of The West and Lag of The Rest.* (America Economic Review Vol. 82. No.2. May 1992. Pp. 162-167). Used by permission.

Questions

1. How did the African slaves contribute to the wealth of Europe?
2. According to this case, how did Europe underdevelop Africa?
3. Why do you think the African leaders concentrated on enslaving their fellow colleagues rather than development of the continent?
4. "The treasures captured outside Europe by undisguised looting, enslavement and murder flowed back to the mother-country and were turned into capital there." Discuss this statement.
5. Elaborate on the statement "Here was the 'original sin' that began the partition between the rich and the poor regions."

CASE STUDY 2.2

THE MASTER FARMERS' SCHEME IN NYASALAND, 1950-1962: A STUDY OF A FAILED ATTEMPT TO CREATE A "YEOMAN" CLASS

THE AUTHOR, OWEN KALINGA, IS IN THE HISTORY DEPARTMENT AT THE UNIVERSITY OF THE WESTERN CAPE, AND THE RESEARCH UPON WHICH THIS CASE IS BASED WAS CONDUCTED IN MALAWI BETWEEN 1985 AND 1989. EARLIER VERSIONS OF THE PAPER WERE PRESENTED AT THE 34TH ANNUAL CONFERENCE OF AFRICAN STUDIES ASSOCIATION OF THE UNITED STATES OF AND AT THE AFRICAN STUDIES SEMINAR, UNIVERSITY OF CAPE TOWN.

IT IS GENERALLY ACCEPTED that following World War II the British Government impressed upon governors in the tropical colonies the need to concentrate upon agriculture so as to increase the production of food crops. Policy makers in Whitehall were convinced that the solution to some of the domestic problems, especially those of a social-economic nature emanating directly from the war, lay in the colonies. Such problems included inadequate supplies of food which, it was feared, would lead to poor nutrition, low productivity and ultimately to serious unemployment. Using mechanisms provided by the Colonial Development and Welfare Act of 1940, funds were made available for projects on the latter expand agriculture.[1] The weight and urgency placed on the latter inevitable led to greater government intervention in production processes and in the marketing of commodities. But perhaps of more significance was the manner in which the new approach to problems involved fairly determined attempts to reshape African societies. As Frederick Cooper has demonstrated so well, the central issue became that of 'order and control' not in urban areas, nor in the workplace in industry and settler-dominated commercial farming, but also in rural situations where peasant production had hitherto dominated. Through education and social change it was hoped to establish a different work ethic, even in peasant agriculture.[2] More agriculture experts were to be recruited and a major effort was to be put into the emergence of 'progressive' -- primarily rural based -- farmers who were to be the vanguard of food production.

In almost all British colonies in East and Central Africa, the nurturing 'progressive' farmers became official policy during the 1940s and 1950s: in Kenya there were the Land Consolidation Programme of 1953 and the Swynnerton Plan of 1954 both of which were intended to advance the development of independent farmers; in Northern Rhodesia there was the African Farming Improvements Scheme (A.F.I.S.O.) mainly in the southern and eastern provinces; and similar projects existed in Uganda and Tanganyika.[3] All these schemes were undoubtedly directed at improving agriculture but they were also aimed at political stability since it was always hoped that the new type of farmers could be relied upon to support the colonial governments, especially in the light of the rising tide of African nationalism. But this economic solution to a political problem achieved varied results which generally depended on local circumstances.

This [case]* discusses the evolution in Nyasaland of such an agricultural project, the Master Farmers' Scheme, and assesses its effectiveness in food production and in the creation of an elite class of farmers. Although the Master Farmers experiment touches on many issues, this [case] will examine it at four contextual levels only, namely, agriculture and development ideas in post-war Africa, transformation of production, growth of rural differentiation and, finally, rural protest and resistance which in this particular case was affected by the changing realities of a colony which throughout the 1950s was part of the Federation of the Rhodesias and Nyasaland.

Originally, denotes paper

Policy and its implications

In response to the post-war appeal from the Colonial Office to step up food production, the Nyasaland Government considered a number of options. Various agricultural schemes were proposed, peasant production was re-examined and there was revival of agricultural co-operatives which in the pre-war period had not been taken seriously. In addition to this the Master Farmers project, aimed at encouraging the development of a distinct group of 'yeoman' farmers, was planned. Although initially proposed in 1946 the project was not executed until after the disastrous famine of 1949 which affected most of the country.[4] To many agricultural and administrative officials in Nyasaland the famine had, among other things, proved the ineffectiveness of peasant production and, because of this, they began to urge the colonial government to give full support to the Master Farmers Scheme which was seen as the answer to African agriculture.[5] Field officers were called upon to identify such African farmers with 'potential' and encourage them to aim at becoming Master Farmers. Registers were kept so as to ensure that, in spite of transfers of field officers, the progress of the farmers could be consistently watched and fostered. The scheme commenced in 1950 and came to an end 1962 when the nationalist government replaced it with the Integrated Rural Development Programme.[6]

The aims of the Master Farmers' Scheme were clearly articulated by the new Director of Agriculture, Richard Kettlewell, a bright and ambitious officer who had been in the service of the Nyasaland government since the 1930s and was to dominate agricultural policy throughout the 1950s.[7] In his long brief Kettlewell argued that the policy of persuading village communities to follow land usage procedures as dictated by government had not succeeded primarily because the majority of communities had continued to live on and cultivate their traditional and rather heavily populated lands which were often misused. It was suggested that for a village community to adopt an accepted land usage system, it would be necessary to rearrange completely individual holdings to allow for easy crop rotation and the establishment of special areas for, among other things, grazing and woodland. This, it was feared, would not be acceptable as the new system would involve reserving some crop land to lie fallow or even to leave it completely unused for restorative purposes. It was further argued that, except in the most favorable circumstances or where a community could be settled afresh on unoccupied land, it was a waste of time and effort to make a deliberate attempt to convert existing trust land to an orderly layout.[8]

Officials were convinced that it was impossible to improve land usage under the existing system and because of this, there was to be a shift of emphasis from the general community to a concentration on a policy designed to evolve and encourage the yeoman farmer enclosing and farming his own land. This, it was hoped, would lead to effective land use and to better living standards for those involved. Those who could not succeed under this system could seek employment in other fields and this would lead to 'a landless class whose work will be better for absolute dependence upon the fruits of it'.[9] It was also pointed out that earlier efforts at encouraging the emergence of individual farmers had not achieved the desired results mainly because 'the minimum requirements of good farming have appeared too revolutionary to find acceptance with no more certain reward than the verbal assurance that they will pay.'[10] Such efforts had also failed because of the requirement that a farmer had to set aside some land to lay fallow, and some individuals had not considered this as particularly beneficial. Kettlewell also argued that, as community spirit had broken down, there was not stimulant to assist in removing individual fears and prejudices and thus the future of agriculture in the colony lay with the encouragement of the best individuals.

To ensure that the envisaged 'yeaman farmer' really emerged, the Master Farmers' Scheme was to be given a boost by the introduction of bonus payments for those who were to 'farm their land in conformity with prescribed conditions'.[11] The bonus payments were viewed not only as an incentive to good agriculture but also as compensation for accepting the rotation system which involved resting a portion of their cropland at regular intervals. Under the scheme there were to be two categories of farmers, First Class and Second Class, each with its own rate of bonus which was to be paid every until 1958 when the scheme would reviewed. The conditions for qualifying as class A and B master farmers were essentially the same although those governing the former category were stricter and more demanding.

Seven conditions applied to both classes of farmers: (i) scattered holdings had to be consolidated into one block of a minimum of ten acres, although the Provincial Agricultural Officer (P.A.O.) might recommend a smaller holding as long as it was not less than four acres; (ii) such conservation methods as prescribed by the Natural Resources Ordinance had to be followed; (iii) all good farming rules and practices relevant to the locality and to be followed; (iv) a minimum of one third of the consolidation holding had to be under grass, pigeon peas or fallow (excluding regeneration scrub) for at least three years -- the P.A.O. could waive the condition involving the resting of a portion of the holding as long as four course rotation (including one leguminous crop and one leguminous green manure break) was adopted; (v) a piece of land could not be cultivated for more than five consecutive years; (vi) all produce land had to have adequate storage facilities and, for a tobacco farmer, reasonable curing barn accommodation had to be provided; (vii) farmers were to be urged to grow timber on their holdings.[12]

Those farmers aspiring to the first class category had to fulfill additional conditions mainly relating to animal husbandry. Farmers had to ensure proper care and housing for all livestock, and this would involve adequate bedding and feeding during the cold season. The farm and field where the livestock lived to be hedged and a section of the farm had to be manured and, in cases where there were no livestock, 'reasonable quality of good quantity compost [had to] be made and applied to the land.' First class aspirants were also to be encouraged to grow fruits and vegetables although this was not regarded as an essential condition. The veterinary department would be prepared to assist farmers in building better houses for animals and farmers could buy carts at subsidized prices. Cash loans would also be available from Native Authority funds for farmers to purchase capital equipment including stock, carts and ploughs.[13]

The onus of identifying potential master farmers lay with the agricultural field officers, some of whom had already identified such farmers. Individuals with carts were to be preferred as 'they were not only usually men of substance but already possess the most important implement for farming and, presumably, trained oxen as well'. Traditional rulers were to be consulted in the selection of farmers and were to be 'kept informed of their progress.' [14]. However, the criteria to be applied by traditional rulers were not spelt out. Farm schools were to be established in the three provinces of the country and farmers would periodically go to these institutions for practical training. Agricultural officers were strongly advised to establish confidence and good relations between them and the farmers. They were also warned not to push the farmers into undertaking improvement in every direction at once.[15]

The planners of the scheme did not consider whether under the existing tenure system a farmer could be assured of security over rights of land. Indeed, concern was expressed in some quarters that Africans would not put much effort, time and expense into the development of land, the tenure of which remained insecure. Security of land tenure was particularly important in areas where the matrilocal system of marriage was practiced and where, therefore, a man had to reside at his wife's home and, as often happened, could be asked to return to his own village upon the dissolution of the marriage or upon the death of his wife. It was proposed that the problem might be alleviated if emphasis could now be placed on a family or village unit instead of an individual.[16] Firmer of land, it was pointed out, were important, especially that larger units of land would evolve accompanied by a 'landless class of laborers'. It was envisaged that such developments would of necessity require an improvement in social services to ensure that, upon retirement, the laborers would not become destitutes as they would have family gardens to depend on. [17]

It is was not clear how the land class which was expected to emerge would find work in the country. Furthermore the consolidation of all scattered holdings into one block was not practical as long as the government had not laid down a definite policy on the machinery and procedure on this and related issues. Officials such as Faulkner, the Director of Veterinary Services, preferred 'the application of communal or co-operative principles to African development schemes' which, they argued, were not discriminatory.[18] Agricultural co-operative societies were being encouraged at that time and by the early 1950s there were more than twenty-five registered societies. Officers such as Faulkner would have liked the less elitist agricultural co-operatives to have been used as channels for rural development.

There were other problems with the assumptions of Kettlewell and some of his officials. The basis of the argument that community spirit had broken down and was being replaced by individualism, which the Master Farmers' project would assist to develop further, is not clear. Even though some officers came to believe that western education and a money economy had made inroads into community life, there is no evidence to suggest that this was indeed the case. As Van Velsen has convincingly demonstrated, the Lakeside Tonga, who of all Malawi peoples were the most exposed to western education through the Livingstonia Mission and Bandawe and who were also to be the leading labor migrants in Nyasaland, did not lose their community spirit. Indeed, if anything, western education, which in their case was almost always followed by labor migration, tended to perpetuate the traditional community identity.[19] Watson's work on the Mambwe of northern Zambia came to the same basic conclusion.[20] It is clear that Kettlewell and some of his colleagues were keen to see the development of a society in which there were the 'haves' and the 'have-not', the rural and the urban, the employers and the laborers, the proletariat and the bourgeois. It was presumed that having been tutored in 'proper' agriculture and conservation this new breed of law abiding farmers would prosper and become employers of the new landless, some of whom would join the work force on European-owned farms which were experiencing a labor shortage at the time.[21]

Meantime, field officers had already begun to identify potential Master Farmers and, where possible, officers made visits to such farmers to discuss the scheme. The farmers were told that lack of capital would not be an impediment as they could easily obtain loans from the Native Authority treasuries, and that with these they could buy cattle, carts and ploughs and be assisted in clearing land for the development of their farms. Lists of potential Master Farmers were compiled and, by 1955, some of them had qualified in the 1st class and 2nd class categories. The agricultural supervisor at Domasi reported with some satisfaction that at the end of 1955 there were three full Master Farmers and twelve potential ones, and that the farmers had received their bonuses as laid down in the ruler.[22] Similarly in 1954 the Provincial Agricultural Officer for the Northern Province referred to an encouraging number of potential farmers and, by the middle of 1955, he was requesting bonus payments for eighteen farmers, seven in the First Class category and the remainder in the lower one. The same reports came from the central region, especially from districts such Kota Kota, Salima and Dowa.[23]

Most of the people who had joined, or were eager to become part of, the Master Farmers' Scheme seem to have had some capital even before the introduction of the project. Some were village headmen or chiefs and, therefore, had a salary, albeit small, and certainly through their position such traditional rulers had acquired property which could be used as security for loans. For example, in Zomba district the first three 'potential' Master Farmers who were 'slowly being groomed' by field officers were all village heads. They were village headwoman Tawakili of Chikowi,
village headman Disi of Kuntumanji and group village headman KuNamondwe. All of them were later confirmed as fully-fledged Master Farmers. The majority of the farmers had worked in the civil service and firms both within the country and outside it and, through retirement benefits, had initial capital with which to invest in farming. Another Zomba farmer, Kumakanga, was a western educated man with a grocery and fish ponds, and was a leading politician in the southern province.[24] Of the numerous northerners who between 1953 and 1956 had written to express their interest in the scheme, three-quarters had already retired or were about to retire from various jobs in Northern Rhodesia and Tanganyika.[25] It is evident, therefore that the Master Farmers' Scheme tended to assist the people who already had the means, and that those without capital of their own found it difficult to join the scheme. Thus a category of farmers was being created from those who had joined or were in the process of joining the petty bourgeois class.

As more people became Master Farmers two issues, both related to acquisition of land and security of its tenure, emerged. Let us start with the latter. Having invested much in their ventures, some farmers were now concerned that, as the land they had cultivated was held under customary law, they could lose it should traditional authority so determine. Such farmers began to demand that the government should confirm their rights to their holdings.[26] The government's answer was to encourage the farmers to obtain leasehold titles in the same way as some missions and trading companies had previously done, but it also advised them to seek the permission of their traditional rulers before taking such action.
Leasehold would involved land being surveyed and beaconed followed by a submission of the Land Application Forms to the district

headquarters. Besides being a long and expensive process, the leasehold system would not be welcomed by traditional rulers as it would directly interfere with a majority aspect of their patronage, that of controlling the distribution of land in their areas. Thus the threat of the application of leaseholds was bound to cause tension between prospective farmers and their chiefs, and also to force people to have a cautious attitude towards the Master Farmers' Scheme thereby hampering its progress. Those who were unhappy with the scheme joined a large number of Africans who were generally opposed to post-famine enforced agriculture and conservation measures.[27]

Officials seem to have been aware of the consequences of introducing leaseholds but they thought that it was a necessary step towards the evaluation of a 'yeoman' farmers class. As the Provincial Agricultural Officer for the Southern Province put it, 'the more title is given to the African cultivator, the less influence the mwini dziko (the owner of the land i.e. the chief) would have on the allocation of gardens and, in breaking down this custom, we would be contributing greatly to a more stable system of land tenure on a peasant basis'. [28] This is certainly an example of engineering social change to suit the designs of government officials, particularly those policy makers such as Kettlewell who viewed African tradition and custom as impediments to the introduction of new measures. There were more cautious officials, however, who argued that for the Master Farmers' Scheme to succeed, title to a farmer's holding should be given not by government but by traditional rulers, thus ensuring that there was no deviation from customary law and practices.[29] Thus the discourse was not only about how to create a respectable African capitalist farmer but it was also about the place of tradition and custom in the new society.

The other problem arising from the introduction of the scheme was the central requirement that each farmer had to have a minimum of eight acres. This was possible in the northern and central provinces where, generally, there was adequate land to enable most farmers to extend their holding populated Southern Province, where land was a problem, prospective farmers were sometimes lucky to get hold of even six acres. To ensure that prospective farmers in the province were not discouraged by the eight acres pre-requisite, it was decided that in special cases a minimum of four acres should be allowed. But even more difficult problem was the requirement that Master Farmers had to consolidate their holdings so that the land under their stewardship was in one block. The consolidation of their land holdings would not be a problem in areas where there was adequate land. Farmer Byron Tembo of Mzimba in the north, for example, had no problems extending his holdings to 45 acres.[30]

In other areas such as Dowa in the Central Province, intending Master Farmers with land scattered in various places had successfully negotiated an exchange of their gardens located elsewhere for additional land next to their holding. However, this was not possible everywhere. Even in Dowa itself thirty to forty per cent of the applicants failed to negotiate, leading to their disqualification. This explains why there were few Master Farmers in densely populated and very fertile areas such Mponela. Where Master Farmers were also village headmen or chief, eni-dziko, the question of additional land, was not always a major issue as often they had already possessed the required acres and thus could easily negotiate for an extension of their holdings.[31] In the Southern Province, the reorganization and extension of holdings was not always a practical propositions and, because of this, the government did not insist on it. The matter of titles and consolidation of holdings was generally a difficult one and, because it was not resolved, the government decided to leave each case to be settled on its own merit.

Meantime, the number of Master Farmers was growing. By 1956 there were 51 farmers in the south, 98 in the centre and 31 in the north. The bonus paid to the farmers had to increase correspondingly, and this caused some alarm among certain government officials in the Secretariat. There was talk of an increased 'snowball effect'. It will be recalled that bonus was to be paid to farmers as a compensation for the land lying fallow and, as the estimates below show, the money was small:[32]

	1954 (est)	1955(est)	1956(est)
Northern Province	96	435	1,100
Central Province	286	1,700	2,500
Southern Province	58	300	400
	440	2,435	4,000*

*All the figures are in pound sterlings.

The Department of Agriculture did not see cause for concern as, according to the 1952 proposal, the bonus programme would ran for four years only. It was further argued that as the scheme was just getting established it would be wrong to stop bonus payments to new entrants before the 1957 season when it was due for review.[33]

Surveys of the performance of Master Farmers were carried out in 1955 and 1956, and it is clear from the data collected that the scheme was proving unprofitable to the farmers. In the 1954/55 season Byron

Tembo had thirty-one acres, sixteen of which were under cultivation. Of the latter, ten acres were planted with maize and the remainder with groundnuts and according to the Provincial Agricultural Officer of the north, the maize crop was valued as 46s** an acre totaling 43; while at 7s an acre the groundnuts has a total value of 44 2s 6d. After taking into account labor costs involving stumping, planting, weeding, harvesting and wages for headers, and other costs such as the value of unsold crops, Tembo made a loss on his farm of 20 13s. However, as a first grade Master Farmers, Tembo received a bonus of 62 on his thirty-one acre farm. This meant that he made a farming profit of 41 8s 6d which went up when the 10 profit from his trading store is added.[34] There can be doubt therefore that the bonus was responsible for Tembo's profit that season.

Byron Tembo had invested much in the initial development, especially in the stumping of his land. He had also to pay back loan and was anxious to purchase another cart. Unfortunately he had problems selling his maize because, as a result of the reduction of markets by the Maize Control Board, he had no buyers for his produce. In spite of this, agricultural officials were optimistic about Tembo's future as a farmer. It was expected that after finally developing his holding and, depending on the availability of produce markets, he would expect a clear annual profit of 30, that is, without the bonus. This figure was likely to rise to 40 if he planted more groundnuts and tobacco than maize. It was feared, however, that the entry into tobacco farming might reduce the projected figure adversely. It was hoped that when his food (from the farm) was considered, his annual percentage profit might be assessed as 15 percent of his capital assets.[35]

An examination of the accounts of seven farmers in the Dowa-Lilongwe-Ntshisi area shows as similar pattern. The holdings of the seven farmers ranged between 12.8 and 39.4 acres, and all of them grew tobacco as well as maize, groundnuts and beans. Their income from maize was slightly higher than that of the northern farmers largely because marketing board had well established markets such as Madisi, Mitundu, Mpingu, Nambuma and Mponela, all which were also linked to feeder markets in the remoter areas. The income of these central province farmers, some of whom regarded the Master Farmers Scheme as a mere extension of their agriculture activities, was further enhanced by the sale of tobacco which at that time was easily then most profitable cash crop. When labor costs, the hire of carts and equipment, the value of produce not sold or retained for food and seed are considered, their income was reduced only to be boosted by bonuses which ranged between 11 and 56.[36]

The picture of the Master Farmers in the Zomba and Blantyre districts of the Southern Province was slightly different from the Central and Northern situations. The Zomba and Blantyre farmers tended to have less land than their counterparts in the other two provinces and, therefore, they received lower bonuses. However, in the 1955/66 seasons, their profit was the highest, ranging between 56 and 75 a year. The main reason for this is that the principal crops grown were maize, beans, peas, and potatoes, all of which were in great demand in the urban centres of Zomba and Blantyre-Limbe. Some southern farmers incurred losses which were directly attributable to the fact that labor costs in the province were the highest in the country.[37]

So the Master Farmers' Scheme has a limited success in that it had aroused interest in the minds on many farmers and also had introduced some of them to modern methods of agriculture.
However, the scheme has not succeeded in showing that the application of such methods could pay dividends: as the few angro-economic surveys of 1955 and 1956 had demonstrated, without their bonuses most farmers would not benefit from joining the scheme. Furthermore it was clear that the employment of manual labor of 'African crops' tended to result in a loss to the farmer. In the view of some farmers this, added to the low prices levels and to the unavailable of good markets, was turning the scheme into a liability. Many farmers were continuing to depend on pensions as well as canteens, brick-making and other income generating activities to sustain agriculture. In other words they were 'straddlers', continuing to engage in off-farm employment. Some field officials began to appreciate this and even recommended that, as the bonus payment was disguising the real profit of the farmers, it should be re-examined. The feeling was that the bonus was not necessarily conducive to good farming; that farmers of less that eight acres ought to be excluded from it; and that material bonuses such as ox-carts and livestock should be considered instead of the financial one. It was also suggested that easier long term loans for initial capital improvement were likely to prove more helpful that bonuses.[38]

As originally planned, the Master Farmers' project was reviewed in 1957 and, as expected, the main change was in the area of the bonus. From that time onwards, bonus payments had to be spent on specific improvement in the area. It was hoped that this innovation would lead 'towards dependence upon loans with similar ties and conditions which will take the place of the bonus scheme when it comes to an end'.
Under the revised rules, 'improved' fallow land was to qualify for bonus payments, and this meant excluding bush fallow: only land

planted with grass, pigeon peas or any other approved restorative crop
now qualified.

Furthermore, although three years would remain as the period for
bonus payments, a Second Class farmer had the chance of a fourth
year during which he could qualify for the first Class category. A
prospective Master Farmer had to satisfy the field officer that his farm
could reasonably be expected to produce subsistence for himself and
his family, besides a cash income of not less than 60 pounds per
annum; this meant that a farmer's holding could not be less than about
eight acres.[39]

The importance of the Master Farmers' Scheme was once again
stressed by the Director of Agriculture who also appealed to his field
staff, especially the African instructors to devote most of their time to
the project. As he put it, 'there are few things more satisfying to the
agriculturist than to see results from his efforts in the shape of a lot of
farmers doing their land well and becoming prosperous and contented
as a results'.[40]   Kettlewell remained steadfastly committed to the
project.

**Tighter legislation, punitive measures and their effects on the
scheme.**

A year before the 1957 review took place, legislation had been
passed to enable agricultural officials to prosecute farmers, including
those outside the Master Farmers' Scheme, who were not following the
proper methods of agriculture. People came to be prosecuted for
bundling offenses; for not clearing their gardens early; and even for
poor crops spacing and late weeding.[41] Special agricultural inspectors
paid visits to farms and if they noticed a laxity in the application of
rules, the offenders were summoned to their chief's court where almost
invariably a fine was imposed on them. In their 1956 season 8,107
people in the Southern Province were prosecuted, and over 230
farming offenses were committed in the North.[42] In 1957 agricultural
inspectors were instructed to be more selective in their prosecution but
courts were expected to impose stiffer fines on offenders. As expected,
the number of cases taken to court decreased but the money paid as
fines increased remarkably. Bundling fines, for example, went from
between 5s and 10s to between 4 and 9 pounds. In some instances
farmers were fined as much as 15 pounds.[43]

Not unnaturally the prosecutions and the accompanying increase in
fines were not welcomed by the farmers and the peasants in general.
Good agriculture was no longer viewed as something to look forward
to. 'Forced' agricultural methods became a focal point of agitation,

and nationalist politicians joined together to support the victims. They argued that education was better than persecution and went on to urge government officials to desist from more punitive action.[44] Some farmers became active politicians in their areas and, threatened by more prosecutions, they began to pay less attention to the advice of agricultural officers, even when such advice was actually sensible. The farmers who continued to co-perate with agricultural field officers were ostracized and referred to as 'stooges' and 'sell outs'. As the political climate in the country changed following the return from exile in July 1958 of Dr. H.K. Banda, tension between some farmers and government official increased. The farmers-cum-politicians were not seen as subversives who had come to align themselves with the nationalists who were agitating for the overthrow of the colonial government. For their part, the farmers looked upon officials as oppressors. During the 1959-60 country-wide state of emergency, some farmers were detained and the supervision of agriculture almost came to a halt.[45] Except for the punitive aspects, the results of the 1957 review of the Master Farmers' Scheme had hardly been implemented.

Rural protest against unpopular agricultural regulations was neither new nor peculiar to Nyasaland. Earlier, the post-famine conservation measures had led to country-wide discontent culminating in the Ntcheu (Ncheu) and Choo (Thyolo) disturbances in 1953.[46] In Tanganyika similar government regulations led to protests which contributed immensely to the spread of the Tanganyika African National Union, the nationalist party formed in 1954.[47] Enforced agriculture rules are also well documented in Northern Rhodesia. Indeed, the issue of the correlation between peasant protesters and nationalist politics has occupied historians of that country in recent years and, inspite of the apparent divergence of views, there is a general agreement among scholars that: (i) the Zambian African National Congress (later the United National Independence Party) tended to draw support from the peasants who, throughout the colonial period, had suffered from variety of agrarian-related laws, and that for them therefore the protest of the 1950s were merely a continuation of their struggles; (ii) that there were farmers who were involved in the government sponsored projects resented the manner in which the regulations were enforced;[48] (iii) that leadership of the nationalist parties, although fairly conservative in such cases, assumed a radical stance to convince the peasants and middle peasants that they could champion their cause effectively.

The Northern Rhodesia analysis just summarized can easily be applied to Nyasaland in the 1950s. However, there are some observations to make which are relevant to our understanding of the antagonism towards the Master Farmers' Scheme during that period.[49] It is important to appreciate that no significant study has been carried out on rural protest in Nyasaland in the late 1940s and 1950s to enable us to establish the nature of linkages between peasant struggles and nationalist politics at that time. We are certain though that some of the prominent producers of food -- especially those outside the agricultural projects -- became influential in their communities and that, as the anti-colonial feelings heightened in different parts of the country, many of them became active members of the Nyasaland African Congress, the organization which was behind the strong opposition to the establishment of the Federation of Rhodesia and Nyasaland.[50] The Master Farmers' Scheme and those in it began to be associated with the Federation. According to one explanation, Congress led a campaign, mostly in the rural areas, to isolate the Master Farmers on the grounds that as property owners, a major qualification for registering on the voters roll, they could be used by government to support an institution which was much disliked by Africans in the three territories. Master Farmers were therefore characterized as the betrayers of a major nationalist cause.[51]

At face value this reasoning appears simplistic and unconvincing, especially when it is not known how many committed Master Farmers were to the creation of the Federation. However, the conflict between the Master Farmers and Congress can be looked as the a competition between aspiring capitalists, one supported by government, the other independent. Each was engaged in accumulation, a process which often involves acquiring influence, itself often competitive. As already pointed out, many leaders of Congress at national and local levels were businessmen engaged in activities such as shopkeeping, brick making and commercial farming (especially those in Central and Southern provinces who were involved in tobacco from the early 1930). Others were property owners in townships and the peri-urban areas of Zomba, Blantyle-Limbe and Lilongwe; other still were influential members of the co-operative societies whose management often abused its responsibilities by, for example, misusing assets.[52] Although many people in this category had chosen not to join the government-backed projects, they viewed Master Farmers with suspicion and jealousy. At a certain level therefore, this unpopularity of the Master Farmers' Scheme in the 1950s was a manifestation of intra-class struggles.

It is also true however, that at another level this was a case of an internally divided peasantry. Through the Master Farmers' Scheme, some had moved up the social-economic ladder and begun to articulate interests which were different from the peasants whose status had not changed. Even though most Master Farmers could not be described as affluent, they had easier access to scarce resources than the average villager. Among such resources were loans and bonuses, agricultural implements and chemical fertilizers. Such privileges only served to emphasize the differences between rural producers and also to exacerbate the tension between them.

Some agricultural officers realized that punishment for not following good agricultural practices such as bundling was unproductive and that, if it the enforcement of agricultural rules was not relaxed, field officers would become totally ineffective. They had to work with farmers and, as one official put it, 'the removal of our field staff of the responsibility of enforcing the regulations will, after the initial deterioration of the standards of conservation, enable us to become agricultural advisors, and it is my personal belief that this is the only way in which we can look for long-term progress.[53] Another officer, Ambrose, even suggested that the government should encourage the evolution of 'non-governmental African bodies which have a vested interest in the proper execution of measures that to many of their contemporaries seem merely irksome and unnecessary restrictions'. Such bodies would have the responsibility of explaining policy to the rural population. Ambrose concluded:

> Paternalism as a method of colonial administration may be sound if the modern doctrine of freedom of expression for the 'child' does not become the vogue. Once that has happened, and it has happened in Nyasaland, paternalism is out, and a more indirect method for putting desirable measures into effect has to be worked out.[54]

Such views were not in vogue in 1958-60 and they were not welcome in government circles during the state of emergency.

**All figures are in pounds.
Source: Owen Kalinga. *The Master Farmers' Scheme in Nyasaland, 1950-1962: A Study of Failed Attempt To Create a "Yeoman" Class. (African Affairs)*. Volume 92. No. 368. July 1993. Used By Permission.

Questions

1. What are four major factors that influenced the start of the Master Farmers project?
2. What were the seven conditions which the farmers had to fulfill and how well did they do this?

3. What does Kettlewell's assumption about African individualism tell you about his approach to the whole project?

4. Who among the Africans was willing to join the Master Farmers project?

5. Why did some farmers want their own land rights as opposed to government controlled land?

6. What is your overall impression about Master Farmers project? What went wrong and how could the situation have been improved?

8. Assess the colonial administration method of leadership in this project and similar projects in Africa. What were the major strengths and weaknesses?

Chapter Three

DEMOCRACY: CAN IT EXIST IN AFRICA?

Democracy has become a common term among professionals, politicians, and even non educated citizens. It has become so common that it carries various definitions. Groups have used democracy as a tool of offense. Governments especially in Third World countries have used the term to suppress opposing groups so have the opposing groups. In the rural areas if one seeks the meaning of democracy, he or she is amazed by different "definitions". In the cities, the term has more diverse usage. Mob justice will kill in the name of democracy. A government misusing public funds will say this was done in an effort to achieve democracy. Recurring confusion has evolved as the media and the public come up with new meanings to democracy. This raises the questions,"is democracy all that it is said to be?" Who among these groups is right, and practicing democracy? Is there a form of democracy that is ideal for Africa and the world at large? This chapter aims at bringing some light to this crucial topic.

THE SOURCES OF DEMOCRATIC IDEALS

The origins of Western tradition from which Britain and the United States derive their ideals and practices of government   started with Greek political thought and structure, five centuries before the beginning of Christianity. Many significant features of the tradition come from Hebrew thought introduced to the West by Christianity. The effect and influence of Christianity continued for over a century before the beginning of the modern age. The result was a remarkable synthesis in the political thought of the middle ages.

Democratic ideas evolved over centuries. The evolution has faced challenges and various changes that have led to modern democracy. It took over four hundred years of thought development and reflection on different ideals to formulate and come up with the modern democratic ideals   established in both Britain and United States. The major emphasis on this development has been individual liberty. This explains why democracy is the liberty of democratic ideals -- probably that is why people refer to themselves as liberated in democratic societies.

THE IDEAL OF DEMOCRACY

The central idea of democracy is its emphasis on the well-being of man and freedom. Democracy has emphasized individual freedom, social order, and equality. These elements, however, have been expensive in terms of time, money, life and social crisis.

Democracy aims at satisfying man through identifying him as worthwhile and important. J. Corry, in his book *Elements of Democracy Government* (1951) notes:

> The ideals of democracy government, that is, government controlled by the people for their purposes, must be widely accepted and believed by people or those ideals cannot, by definition, be democratic. Respect for individual personality is the maxim on which it has been possible to get widespread agreement (p. 24).

By committing itself to the most crucial element of life, individual personality and freedom, democracy has flagged a single message over the years. Even before the Christian era, the Stoic philosophers in Greece promoted the importance of brotherhood of men. The fact that man · belongs to a common humanity that makes him a member of a common race has generated the ideal even further. "They urged the duty of the individual to realize Truth and Goodness in his own life, to enlighten the understanding of his fellows by precept and example, and to attest his faith in human dignity by succoring the unfortunate" (p. 26).

Democracy has borrowed much of its foundation from Christianity. The central features of the Christian message are the infinite worth of the individual soul, the denial of all distinctions of rank or place, and the redemption of mankind through grace and love. Christianity asserted the importance of individual responsibility to God, and the necessity of rendering an account of his stewardship at the last judgment. In the final balance of the soul, duty to the earthly king would not be an excuse for failing in the service of God. While Christianity admits that Caesar deserves his due, it is not Caesar who sits at the last judgment, thus religious duty has a higher claim than any earthly authority.

Although the ideal democracy has a secular origin, it has a powerful religious connection for its main tenets. The very core of democracy is the same core for Christianity. Christianity believes that responsibility of the individual to God gives strong support to the claims for individual freedom. It also calls for a large measure of social equality and challenges the gap between the rich and the poor.

The primary concern of democracy is the establishment of order and security that is adequate for the free development of personality. Democracy expresses a faith that if men are secure in their persons, they will in turn treat each other with respect and dignity. This leads to love for one another and promotion of friendship. As the saying goes, "friends don't demand justice because that justice is freely available to all."

WHEN IS DEMOCRACY DEMOCRATIC?

Governments may claim they are democratic but that does not make them so. A democracy is not a democracy unless it responds to the will of the people. It is a government not feared by its people who have much confidence in its operations and electorate procedures. Dictatorship forms of governments have leaders and small cliques around the heads who decide the governments' operations and decision making process. In such a government, the leaders are able to act rapidly and maintain consistency in their leadership because they have only a few minds to consult and convince. In a democratic government, decisions are difficult to make because the ultimate decision about the country's management rests with the millions   who make decisions   through their electorate mandate. The process is cumbersome, and a great amount of time and effort is necessary to consult   the wishes of the sovereign electorate. More important still, it is exceedingly difficult for millions to come to a common mind or a majority decision about anything.

DEMOCRATIC GOVERNMENT

A democratic government is a government instituted in accordance with the will of the people. It is the people who hold major decision-making power through their electorate rights. To accomplish this, however, two qualifications are necessary.

First, government in accordance with the will of the people cannot be taken to mean consultation on every act of government. Rather it must be taken to mean that periodically each member of the electorate is enabled to state his preference between the candidates and the announced policies of two or more political parties. . . If a majority of the electorate is opposed to the policy of the group presently in control of the government, it can change its rulers and bring to power another group of politicians with a policy more to its liking . . . Second, . . . it is the will of majority that prevails as controversial questions. The fact that there is a controversy ensures that some portion of the electorate will be dissatisfied with any decision taken. The will of the people is not the will of all. Even then, the majorities are mustered only occasionally and say their say on only a small fraction of the specific decisions that are taken in the name of government (Beans, 1939:307-308).

In a democratic society, the citizens enjoy the privileges of citizenship. The goal is attainable through voting in elections and freedom of speech. It is a society where members decide an outline of what type of government to install and define its behavior. Such a government reflects society's understanding and interest. Refusing to vote is still democratic. The person refusing to participate in voting is still helping to decide. It is the goal of every person to ensure that the government they choose is the one deserved. The citizens have a key role in influencing their government to reflect their will and desire.

> Citizenship is more than an opportunity: it is also a responsibility. . . . it is not necessary, or even possible, for every citizen to understand the nature and problems of government. But democracy will certainly be a failure unless there comes forward voluntarily in each generation a large number of citizens prepared to give the time and thought necessary to the understanding in political life. By the attitude we take toward this responsibility, we decide the fate of democracy (Corry, 1951:11-12).

To be democratic does not mean satisfying every member of a society. This has never happened and will never happen. However, we need to understand that common ideas set standards for government to follow. A government cannot succeed without getting ideas from those who put it in place. A government can only have credibility if it meets its main aim and has a conviction that its general goal is in line with its record of operations and performance. Lack of support from the citizen is enough to shake a government. Even those brutal governments that keep a significant portion of their population in labor camps and detentions must have some popular support from some people. It may be that the government popularity is through some frauds, but a government cannot succeed without unifying ideas. It may use power to remain in leadership, but its credibility lies with the citizens who score it every day, either as a failure or a success.

DEMOCRACY IN AFRICA

Africa as a continent and its people have always been unstable due to many "winds" which come from all directions, bringing different ideology and politics.

First came the Arabs who for a long time traded with Africans especially from Eastern and Northern Africa. Following the Arabs was demand for slaves to work in big plantations, both in the Far East and Europe. After a long period of slavery that took many strong men and women from Africa, the deadly practice ended toward the end of the nineteenth century. The end of slavery did not mean an end of foreigners to Africa. As soon as slaverly was abolished, missionaries and explorers invaded Africa. Their goal was to open the continent for colonialism. It was after colonialism that Africans realized they had been misused and they revolted, leading to independence for many countries. Although the countries became flag independent, economically, politically and socially, they remained dependent upon the Western nations -- Europe and North America. Some of them also developed strong ties with the former Soviet Union. Little wonder then, that the external influence to Africa had so much impact on the continent. It is not a surprise the same external powers have come up with another ideology known as democracy.

However, the term democracy is not new in Africa. The trend of democracy emphasized today in Africa is different from that which has existed in the past. Like many ideologies in the past, the democracy in Africa today brings another cry -- the need for freedom.

Today, Africa is in a state of political change, the demand for democratization. Since the 1960s, when many countries attained independence, many countries had one party as the ruling party. Toward the end of the 1980s, the demand for democracy persisted in most countries. Uprisings followed, as people have demanded democratic governments. Support for the new move comes from the Western nations. These powers have strongly opposed the existing governments and have demanded instant change in Africa. Such a change of events among the European powers is not a surprise to many in Africa, after all, they support the ideology that is rooted in the same powers. Due to many restrictions and conditions, both economic and political, the African leaders are forced to call for transition to multi-partism, the key element in democracy. The most troubled countries are those south of the Sahara desert. In Central Africa, for example, both Congo and Gabon have experienced the pressure. In Zaire and Rwanda, pressure to change has also increased. The same trend has spread to East, South and Western Africa. The pressure to submit to democracy is amazingly widespread. Apart from Botswana that held multi-party elections since independence the list   of countries demanding true democracy has increased   on an annual basis. Through much pressure, several countries have given in to multi-party elections or have promised to do so. Among them are Angola, Benin, Cameroon, the Comoros, Congo, Ghana, Madagascar, Mozambique, Rwanda, South Africa, Togo, Zambia, Cote d'Ivoire (former Ivory Coast), Kenya and Zaire.

The acceptance of multi-party elections was not a one day event. The African governments had been in control for over three decades.

This meant that the advocated changes to democracy were challenging and difficult to accept. Strong suppression, violence, and political unrest faced many of the countries. In some countries, many people have died during the process. This wind of democracy has caused differences and conflict of interest in many countries, sometimes leading to civil wars or fear among different ethnic groups. With the process of democratozation being far from completion, it seems many people will die unless there is a peaceful process in the transitions. This is possible as was seen in some countries like Kenya and Zambia during their first multi-party elections. A peaceful transition is a mutual approach to change and shows maturity among the Africans.

WHAT HAS ENFORCED DEMOCRACY?

The governments for decades have ruled under one party system which until recently has been viewed as evil and dictatorial. People who seemed satisfied with their leaders in the past, suddenly rose to demand changes. The demands have taken the form of economic control and media campaigns against the African governments, or certain leaders. Most of the African governments have resisted any indication of loss of power. The effect has been use of different methods to force such governments to accept change.

DONOR POLICY

As discussed earlier, donors have played a key role in the countries' economies and development. They also play key roles in all areas of life -- medical, education, water projects, infrastructure, and government policing. The donors' approach has determined the directions that a country takes. The has made many governments to work together, hand in hand with the donors in order to survive. Donors' practices have not been beneficial to the countries they claim to assist, however.

In the era of multi-party democracy, the donors' role has become a very significant, determining the political climate in the host countries.

Today, many of Africa's major donors are now using their aid policies to pressure governments to practice democratization. For example, during 1990 and 1991, the U.S. Government changed its relations with both Kenya and Zaire to force the countries to have multi-party elections. In Kenya, the United States Congress froze $ 13 million of the $46 million in aid authorized of the 1990 financial year (*Washington Post,* July 10 1990). Similar voices have come from Washington to end military aid to Zaire while constantly supporting democracy and human rights in Africa (*The Sun* April 25, 1990). The same practice of freezing aid was adopted by France and Belgium. The policy affected both Zaire and Gabon. In an article appearing in *New York Times* in 1990, French aid was tied more closely to democratization. And in the same year, "a French threat to suspend its aid allegedly played a critical role in convincing the government in Mali to publicly commit itself to multi-party democracy" (*African Report* 1990: 27).

Britain, which has had much influence in African countries and their   constitutions joined other Western nations in announcing conditions toward foreign aid with a purpose to enhance democracy (*Daily Dispatch,* June 1991). The former Soviet Union support for democratization in Africa came as a surprise to many nations given the communism ideology preached for decades. However, the Soviet support for democralization in Africa was the subject of Shevardnadzes talk with several Africa leaders. (*Soweto* June, 1990).

WHAT EFFECT DOES THE DONORS' CHANGE OF POLICY HAVE ON AFRICA?

According to *African Today's* article entitled "The Changing Global Balance: Outlook for Africa" 1991, the shift in donor policy in favor of democratization is likely to have much greater effect on Africa rhetoric than behavior. "The new policy will be implemented in a period of overall decline in Western Aid " (p.26). Similarly, new strategic interests are likely to emerge to replace those derived from the cold war (p.26).

The donors' actions, backed by their mother countries, have stimulated and motivated the African politicians to look at democratization as the sole solution to African problems. This is especially true in Tanzania where socialism submitted to change to democratization. The socialist government is criticized as responsible for holding back economic development. As a result, "Tanzania has gradually abandoned elements of its socialists experiment in exchange for Western investment and a program of World Bank mandated reforms" (*Africa Today* 1991:22). However, Tanzania was not alone and its neighbor, Zambia, held its first multi-party election in June 1990, which saw its ruling party defeated. The Zambian elections were peaceful, unlike what many had anticipated.

The use of foreign aid restriction as a tool to enforce democracy has been effective in the short run. This is because the Africa countries need foreign aid. The assistance requirement is not only to implement long-term development policies and plans, but to prevent and control immediate and wide-spread famine (*Africa Today* 1991:29). As long as the countries remain needy, any policy adopted by the foreign powers will be effective, at least during the time of need.

At this point, it is important to note that whether with donors' intervention or not, it is difficult to guarantee that a transition to democratic governments will remain peaceful or even successful. According to *Africa Today's* analysis, in both Angola and Mozambique, former Portuguese colonies, the development of democratization systems will first require the settlement of long standing civil wars. Also, in many countries, the regimes are still resisting demands for changes. Most governments fear introduction of many parties could lead to increased ethnic tensions (p.27). As noted earlier, such arguments are critical considering the states' colonial past. As in the former "Soviet Union and Central Europe, reopening the ethnic question in many Africans' minds may be politically akin to opening Pandora's box" (p.27).

CAN AFRICA BE DEMOCRATIC?

The wind of change is hitting Africa like oceanic waves in the name of "true democracy." This indicates a need for some concern. Democratization campaigns and enforcement, when combined with Africa's current economic decline and social crisis need careful attention to avoid considerable instability and civil violence. No one can predict or determine which country or countries will experience political upheaval in the process of democracy restoration. A democracy in Africa must take into consideration the complex cultural factors and social practices that affect the way of life among Africans. Any democracy that neglects any of these elements will not succeed.

A popular definition of democracy is that of Abraham Lincoln. According to Lincoln, democracy denotes a government of the people for the people by the people. The definition shows a great need for participation from all levels in the society. Democracy advocates freedom, liberty, and respect of the electorate. Democracy calls for societal justice and social balance. It advocates consultation of those affected by decisions. True democracy promotes two way communication, both top-down and bottom-up. This allows room for feedback to ensure clear understanding of messages. True democracy means also mutual participation of the parties involved. This kind of democracy is not new in Africa where decisions were made through consultation and discussion by elders, advisers, and priests.

Democracy does not mean that everyone can participate in the process. Only those to be affected need to participate in decision making. It starts from the grass-roots representation to presidential representation.

For true democracy in Africa to be effective, there is need for awareness among all people. People need to learn of the components of democracy before they can apply them. Education is needed to show people what democracy is. Not that they don't understand it, but because there are complications and misuse of the term. As a result, there has been confusion as to what democracy involves and how to carry it out. This includes both the leaders and the public. The West can only be effective if it sincerely aims at helping Africa develop its systems of governments to reflect what is acceptable by all communities. A democracy that takes into consideration a common understanding for all ethnic groups, common understanding of development and its associated problems, common understanding of stages of development thereby aims at a common solution to Africans problems. The West can do a great deal in assisting and making African understand where they may be going wrong. Mutual respect and understanding are necessary. Without such an understanding, African governments and people will keep on going back to where they started leading to more conflict.

Realizing that Africa needs to change its present trend of leadership but with much care, Salim Ahmed Salim, the Organization of African Union (O.A.U) Secretary General noted:

> We have made mistakes. Africa from the very beginning should have addressed itself to the question of conflict. It should have never allowed internal conflict to go unattended. It should never have allowed the violation of human rights to be done with impurity. We had situations

of massive killings in some cases, we have had characters who not only vilified our people and our continent, but got away with murder, and we kept quiet. These were some of the mistakes. We made the mistakes of not putting into concrete action our own commitments in terms of economic cooperation. These are short comings, but now we are trying to overcome these short comings" (*African Report,* 1992:39).

On the wind of change experienced in Africa he observed:

Now that the wind of democratization is sweeping through our continent, my concern -- and I have expressed it during my talks in Washington with Congressmen and administration Officials --is that while the friends of Africa should support this process, the best and most constructive way of doing so is to support Africa in creating institutions for democracy, institutions which can guarantee that the question of democratization is not a whimsical things a passing phase. It does not depend on the likes and dislikes of a particular individual or government, but is something permanent (p. 38).

As expressed by the Secretary General of O.A.U., Africa needs help to build permanent democratic institutions. It is not establishing democracy for them that will assist. It is establishing democracy with them. Emphasizing this point further the Secretary General further commented:

There is a process of democratization taking place in the continent and we understand that the outside world has shown a lot of concern, but really the people who are responsible for change in African countries are Africans themselves. No one, no matter how powerful, how strong, how well intentioned, can actually have democracy created in African society. It has to be the people of that society, taking into account their own social, cultural and historical values (p.38).

To conclude this chapter, let me say that all of us together; Western powers and Africans, can establish democracy in Africa. The Africans themselves must take the initiative while other countries should be willing to work with them in shaping the continent to a desirable environment. African democracy will certainly be different from European, American, Russian, or Asian democracies, since Africans have different cultural, social settings and interpretations of the world. It is the challenge of the West to cooperate with Africans in establishing that democracy that reflects Africa, rather than any other world society. Africa belongs to Africans and they are the ones who know the way to lead their people. Outsiders can help Africans to work out a solution, but will never succeed in solving African problems without involving Africans. American involvement in Somalia proved just how complex the culture and people are to outsiders. Americans had to learn the hard way that they could never solve internal difficulties of another country, in the name of democracy. It just can't work.

CASE STUDY 3.1

THE WHITE MAN'S BURDEN

To grasp the scale of Africa's poverty, consider this statistic: the combined GNP of the entire continent south of the Sahara is less than that of Holland. Worse, Africa is slipping. Sub-Sahara Africa, reported the World Bank earlier this year [1993], "is the only region is the world likely to experience an increase in absolute poverty over the next decade." Worse again, Africa has missed out entirely on the new vogue for private investment in the poor world. For the rest of the decade -- and probably beyond -- it will have to rely for foreign capital almost entirely on aid.

It is bad time to be begging at the rich world's door. [This week] the United states Agency for International Development (USAID) said it was overhauling its entire aid programme and trimming its overseas presence, including that of Africa. The Palestinians have newly joined the East Europeans in the lengthening line of outstretched hands. The World Bank, according to its annual report, published [this week], committed $1 billion less to Africa in the 12 months to June 1993 than in the preceding 12 months. Even Sweden, long a model of generosity, sliced 6% of its aid budget [this year].

Two different trends are clasping Africa in a pincer-like hold. One problem is that rich-world priorities have shifted. The ending of the cold war has eroded the desire to buy friends in Africa. Whenever African leaders gather -- they went [this week] to Virginia to try to drum up black American support -- they fret about "marginalisation": the fact that investors and aid donors from the rich world are losing interest in Africa in favor of the emerging markets or of poverty closer to home.

Such worries are not unfounded. Total aid to Africa, which grew at about 5% a year in the early 1980s, was already stagnating by 1989. In 1991 the net flow of capital (gross flows minus repatriated profits and interest payments: Africa pays back more to the IMF, for example, than it receives) was less than in 1986, in real terms. Brian Atwood, USAID's new head, says his shake-up will not affect the sum of aid for Africa, which is kept distinct from America's general aid pot. But he admits that some missions there will close.

The other grip on the continent comes from the multinational institutions, mainly the World Bank and IMF. The Bank says last year's drop in lending happened because the sums put aside for sub-Saharan Africa in 1992 -- chiefly on account of drought there were unusually high, but there is a more troublesome trend. The Bank increasingly finds itself unable to hand out the cash for African countries embarked on economic reform, because so many fail to meet the target -- shrinking budget deficits, reducing inflation -- agreed with the IMF.

Much of the drop in the Bank's total lending to Africa was due to the absence of lending to Nigeria and Cote d'Ivoire. Both in the past few years have failed to meet the demands of the Fund and the Bank to get their economies into shape. So, aid has been denied. And since IMF support is needed for a country to win debt relief from other credits -- the Fund and the Bank do not write off debts -- the burden on offending countries continues to pile up.

There could be a blessing disguised in this foreign aid squeeze. It is forcing some creditors and donors to reassess what the purpose of their giving should be. Unchecked from cold war needs, can government aid be aimed more purposefully at helping Africas lift themselves out of poverty? Only a tiny share of aid less than 10%, according to UNICEF goes directly to things that help the poor: primary health care, basic literacy and education (especially for women), clean water, family planning.

The World Bank, much disliked in Africa for its economic austerity programmes, has begun to tilt the balance of its own lending this way. Its chief, Lewis Preston, has made a crusade of "poverty reduction".
Though the American government shies away from the word "poverty", Mr. Atwood's shake-up is expected to transform USAID from, in effect, a branch of the state Department. Several European countries are promising to make sure more of their aid reaches Africa's poor.

These are fine words. But will they come true? The World Bank remains handcuffed in its lending by its own tough demands for structural reforms. Good intentions drawn up in Washington or Paris can also get lost on the ground. Oxfam, an aid agency that has worked in Africa for decades, points out that one recent World Bank loan in Mozambique classed as "poverty-targeted" went to a foreign multinational for a project to grow cotton, for which it would be the monopoly buyer. The price it pays, say local Oxfam staff, is half that paid elsewhere.

Though in bilateral aid to Africa grants now outrun loans, the money is rarely an unconditional gesture of generosity. Most is tied to purchases from the donor country: some of this is a thinly disguised direct subsidy to specific contracts. Only five of the 20 top donors, according to a recent report by Action Aid, a British aid agency, tie less than half their aid. France ties 60%, Britain 75%, Italy 90%.

Virtually all American "food aid" goes into buying up America's farm surpluses, chiefly of wheat.

Even those donors that do not officially tie much aid, such as Japan, often reach an official agreements that have the same effect. Limiting the buyer's choice, tied aid in nearly always inefficient. It can also hamper the development of local skills. Oxfam claims that 100,000 consultants from rich countries are now working in Africa, many doing jobs that could be done by Africans.

To spend more aid on what Africa's poorly really need -- rural credit schemes, basic health care -- would, however, mean fewer of the grand infrastructure schemes that so interest the rich world's business lobbies. A likely tale.

Source: *"The White Man's Burden. (The Economist,* London). September 25, 1993. pp. 49-50. Used by permission

Questions

1. What is your opinion concerning donors' reaction toward aid in Africa?

2. Although the donors have been in Africa for over four decades, Africa's state of poverty has worsened. Does this mean the donors have not done their homework?

3. Why should donors shift their interest from Africa to Eastern Europe?

4. "Much of the aid given to Africa never reaches its target." Discuss this statement.

5. If you were a decision maker, working with World Bank or International Monetary Fund (IMF), how would you solve Africa's worse state of poverty?

6. What role do donors play in shaping political structural policies in Africa?

Chapter Four

THE ECONOMY: IS THIS THE SOURCE OF CRISIS IN AFRICA?

Africa is considered to have the potential of being the richest continent in the world. It is a continent with many different resources that she has yet to exploit, for example, oil, iron, and gold. With over forty developing states in Africa, those in the Sub-Saharan region are considered to be poor performers, economically. With a lot of diversity of resources, some countries such as Gabon, Liberia, Tanzania, Mauritania, Nigeria, Zambia, Zaire and Nigeria contain great reserves of minerals which if well utilized could uplift their economies. Other countries such as Kenya, Ghana and Cote d'Ivoire have agricultural products to support their economies. However, according to the world's economic analysts, this continent lags behind all developing countries -- continents such as Asia and South America. The Sub-Saharan states that are considered to be economically poor performers have not demonstrated any significant production either locally or internationally. According to the World Development Report analysis, almost all the countries in the Sub-Sahara region are poor with severe poverty among large parts of the population. The most poverty stricken countries share characteristics typical of all low income countries elsewhere in the world. Even those considered Middle Income countries are much poorer compared with most other World countries in that group.

Table 4.1

SUB-SAHARA AFRICA: SELECTED DEVELOPMENT INDICATORS
(MEDIUM VALUES)

	Low Income Developing Countries		Middle Income Developing Countries	
	Africa	*Others*	*Africa*	*Others*
Income per Person, 1976 (US dollars)	145	155	390	990
Share of Agriculture in GDP, 1976 (percent)	41	47	28	18
Share of Population in Urban Areas, 1975 (percent)	11	18	24	47
Share of Manufacturers in Exports, 1975 (percent)	5	14	5	24
Life Expectancy at Birth, 1975	41	45	44	61
Total Fertility Rate, 1975	6.3	6.2	6.5	5.8
Percentage of primary School Age Children Attending School, 1975	53	51	79	108
Adult Literacy Rate, 1974	23	22	15	72

Source: From *World Development Report 1978* by World Bank. Copyright 1978 by the International Bank for Reconstruction and Development/The Worl Bank. Reprinted by Permission of Oxford University Press, Inc.

African economic growth rates between 1960 and 1975 averaged about 4 percent annually. In 1984, growth declined by 1.2 percent while per capita income declined by 4.2 percent. By 1992, the African economy became a major epidemic because of severe climatic conditions and the worldwide economic recession that lowered the demand for African exports. As a result, Africa was expected to report a negative growth rate. In its recommendation, the 1986 UN Special Session on Africa's Economic Recovery Program had agreed that Africa's success depended on annual external financial flows of $35 billion, but in the subsequent four years, till 1990 the financial flow declined by about 7 percent a year although it continued to export more capital every year than it received by way of aid and loans (Britannica, 1993:355). The gains Africa made were therefore much lower than they had been in the past three decades, a situation expected to worsen in the 1990s.

Today, the current situation in Africa is alarming, both to the world and to the Africans themselves. The declining trend of the economy shows a desperate need of rescuing the continent. With poor economies, poor per capita income, and poor living standards, the question is, why is Africa a victim of suffering? Is there a solution?

Africa And Debt

Compared to other developing countries, apart from Southern Asia, the food production and industrial sectors in Africa remains minimal leading to little benefits from international trade. A continent with resources lagging behind in development is a challenge to those concerned. A rich continent relying on food aid, technical facilities and borrowing as if her people were lazy and handicapped surprises the "world." Today, the African debt crisis is almost beyond her capability. It is almost impossible for Africa to repay these debts, no matter what means she uses. Beside this, there is a sharp increase in debt demand in Africa. Both creditors and debtors were caught unawares as debt rose from US $14 billion in 1973 to $125 billion in 1987 (Whitaker 1988:19).

To show the seriousness of debt crisis in Africa, Karamo N. M. Sonko, in his article *Debt in the Eye of a Storm: The African Crisis in a Global Context,* observes that both short-term and long-term liabilities of Sub-Saharan African countries grew from US $38.5 billion in 1978 to $80 billion in 1984. These figures were less as compared to other parts of the developing world, for example, Brazil and Mexico who each owed over $100 billion individually in 1988. The real magnitude of the Sub-Sahara debt burden is apparent as seen in Table 4.2.

Table 4.2

SUB-SAHARA AFRICA DEBT

Years(US billion)	Debt Service To Exports (%)	Debt to Export (%)	Debt to GDP(%)
1978	3.5	10.0	102.3	24.3
1979	4.4	10.2	96.1	24.5
1980	6.2	10.8	85.0	23.5
1981	6.6	14.2	123.0	29.2
1982	6.8	17.8	177.2	34.4
1983	8.1	22.9	214.5	40.4
1984	10.2	26.9	207.7	41.4
1985	13.0	34.7	217.6	43.4
1986	15.2	39.4	326.3	74.4
1987	8.5	23.8	365.9	101.1
1988	10.0	25.8	340.6	97.7
1989	9.4	20.3	299.9	108.0
1990	10.6	20.6	278.4	107.7

[Source: Carol Lancaster and J. Williamson, *African Debt and Financing.* pp. 28-46 and *World Bank, World Debt of Developing Countries* (Washington, DC. , 1989). Note: The last five figures marked in the last column are the ratios of debt/GNP instead of GDP. 1989 and 1990 figures are estimated and projected, respectively (in *Africa Today,* 1990:16)]. Used by permission of *Africa Today.*

The above table shows that the debt service to export ratio almost quadrupled from 10% ($ 3.5 billion) in 1978 to 39.4% (15.2 billion) in 1986, then falling to 20.6% (10.6 billion) in 1990. The volume of total external debt itself as a percentage of export income tripled from 102.3% in 1978 to 326.3% in 1986. When the desegregated data is examined, the situation becomes even more worrisome. Ezeani has noted that for some countries such as Sudan, Cote D'Ivoire, Mozambique, Madagascar, Mali, Liberia, Guinea Bissau, Togo, Gambia, Comoros, and Equatorial Guinea, debt to GNP ratios exceed 100%, while for others such as Zaire, Zambia, Somali, Chad, and Mauritania, it exceeded 200% (Ebon, 1988:27, in *Africa Today,* 1990:16).

The debt level is alarming both to the countries involved and to donors and creditors. Focusing their eyes on the West for is assistance, the African continent is in a great trap. Africa trapped in a situation that will require a strategic approach to succeed.

Given the current level of economic performance and debt levels, the continent has little hope. If anything, the continent needs more help in terms of loans or "free debts." According to Michael Redclif, the author of *Sustainable Development: Exploring The Contradictions* (1987:69) although the situation in Africa is less severe in terms of the absolute magnitude of the debt, in relative terms the continent is probably worse off. He notes that "in 1983, there were no African countries among the large debtors." Today, to the contrary, the total external debt of the 42 Sub-Sahara economies is in the order of US $ 130-135 billion. "The true average debt-service-to-exports ratio, excluding debt arrears and rescheduling, in these countries was about 35 per cent in 1985" (quoted from Green and Griffith-Jones, 1985). The dilemma is that, put starkly, much of Sub-Saharan Africa is virtually starving while debt interest is being paid (Redclif 1987:69). Most African governments are caught between either assisting their starving population or paying debt. Trying to achieve either has a negative consequence on the other while serving both groups only leads to dissatisfaction of the groups served. Realizing this problem, countries like Germany and Britain have written off outstanding debts for some African counties. Others, like the United States, have decided to assist Africa on conditions of loan repayment or political restructure.

On the basis of the above argument, several questions arise. Why is Africa the poorest performer of all continents? Does this mean the people are different from other continents? Will the continent ever recover? Is it true the continent is the richest as claimed or is this just more propaganda used to make Africa guilty of her progress and contribution to her people and world development? Is there a procedure of developed that can be followed in order to recover? What efforts are Africans making to rectify the situation? These and many other questions need to be answered either directly or indirectly. We can divide the questions into three:

1. Why is Africa the poorest continent economically?
2. What are the Africans doing to rectify the situation?
3. How is the continent preparing for the future challenges?

These three questions look at the causes of the poor economic situation, the solutions sought and the future trends of the continent. The whole process ties the past, the present and the future development of the continent. This is necessary considering attacks

on Africans or Europeans with each group blaming its counterpart as
responsible for the crisis.

WHY IS AFRICA THE POOREST ECONOMIC PERFORMER?

Many theories have been developed to explain these issues. To some
people, Africans are the "cursed" people of the world; Africa is
composed of lazy people; Africans are beggars who borrow and never
give; God designed Africans to be slaves; Africans are inferior while
the Europeans are superior; the location of the continent on earth is
unsuitable for concrete development; and the traditional beliefs and
practices have contributed to lack of commitment: high population,
greed and self-actualization achievable through attainment of power
among different ethnic communities.

While some of the theories may be true, there are no concrete facts
to support them. The truth of any theory can be proved by its
advocates. Such advocates may be biased or the arguments could be
based on wild guesses with few using facts or reliable research. It is
not the objective of this chapter to prove them right or wrong. The
objective is to establish the right trend of thinking and thereby
accept or reject unrealistic theories.

In his effort to explain the reasons for poor performance of the
continent, Douglas W. Lister, in his paper entitled *Africa In The
World Economy*, has noted that in the world economy, Africa has
traditionally played three key roles:

The first role is that of supplying industrial raw materials and
primary agricultural products for the industrial countries; The second
role is that of being a market for the finished and semi-finished
exports of the developed countries; and Finally, that of providing a
field for investment for both public and private firms.

The three roles have been very insignificant when compared to the
roles played by other continents and have not satisfied the Africans.
Africa considers the whole approach dissatisfying in nature and extent
in the world economy and totally unsuitable for the developing
countries (in Knight et. el. 1976: 443). According to Lister, the
problems and dissatisfaction arising have been evident for a long time.
For instance, since 1948, the General Agreement on Tariffs and Trade
(GATT) has regulated the international trade. GATT was originally
designed to bridge the gap between the end of World War II and the

" establishment of an International Agency." However, the agency has grown away from its intended objectives (p.443). Today, the agency has much influence on the world trade system. It has taken and influenced the procedures for disputes' settlement while at the same time, it has been involved in granting waivers. With the help of experts in a given area, the agency has tackled and resolved dozens of trade disputes. To member states, GATT has granted permission to restrict or introduce restrictive measures designed to protect certain sectors, thereby controlling the market. This has enabled these members to have much power upon the custom unions or free trade areas (p. 444).

How has GATT influenced the African economy? The African countries have not been happy with GATT 's operational behavior and its approach to the world economy. One area of concern among the African states has been the Agency's principle of non-discrimination. To the African nations, this principle was incompatible with creation and establishment of infant industries, a situation in which Africa found itself after independence. The African states have also complained of a lack of price controls on primary products. This means that only countries with a lot of production capability, and low costs could dominate the world economy. Besides this, the Africans states complained of being a minority shareholders in major world economic bodies like International Monetary Fund and World Bank (p.448). All these factors ensure a very insignificant role in the World economy, yet GATT plays no key role to rectify the situation (See Table 4.3).

Table 3.3

DIRECTION OF TRADE BY MAJOR TRADING PARTNERS
(U.S. $ MILLIONS AND PERCENTAGE SHARES)

Market	Imports 1974-83	%	Export 1974-83	%
Developed Market Economies	412,535	77	415,145	80
Developing Market Economies	71,945	13	63,700	12
Africa	25,540	5	19,032	2
Total	535,463	100	517,066	100

Source: *The UN, Foreign Trade Statistics for Africa, Summary Tables* (New York, NY, 1986). The percentage shares of Africa and the centrally planned economies are rounded up. (in *Africa Today* 4th Quarter, 1990:19). Used by permission of *Africa Today*.

To date, Africa's performance remains minimal. Her imports exceed exports which shows the continent's continued dependence on outside resources rather than on her own resources.

One major reason given for poor performance of the continent is the production of cash crops. According to Arnold Rivkin, former Development Adviser for International Bank for Reconstruction and Development, and author of *Africa and The West: The African Presence In World Affairs and Nations By Design,* many African states are dependent on the production of a single agricultural product that accounts for 60 percent or more of the states' foreign exchange earnings. Some countries are victims of having a 75 percent dependence on minerals as a source of foreign exchange.

In order to earn foreign exchange needed to make payments on the ever growing debt, African countries have allocated more and more land for export crops like cocoa, cotton, and coffee. Some African nations have oriented their entire agricultural sectors around the production of one or two crops for export. In West Africa, Dahomy depends on palm kernel, Ghana on Cocoa, Gambia on peanuts, Nigeria on oil and palm oil. In East Africa, Somali depends on bananas, Kenya on coffee and tea, while Uganda depends on coffee and copper. In North Eastern Africa, Ethiopia depends on coffee while Sudan relies on cotton. In Central Africa, Zambia depends on copper while Libya to the North depends on petroleum (in Paden at el. 1970:499). This emphasis on export agriculture has cut into the production of food crops for domestic consumption.

Table 4.4

SHARE OF TOTAL EXPORT EARNINGS ACCOUNTED FOR BY PRINCIPLE COMMODITIES

Country Commodities	Principle Percentage
Central Africa	82
Coffee, wood, diamonds	
Chad	80
Cotton, meat, oil	
The Gambia	93
Cocoa, wood, aluminum	
Ivory Cost	61
Coffee, cocoa, wood	
Liberia	81
Iron ore, rubber, coffee	
Nigeria	98
Petroleum, coffee	
Rwanda	82
Coffee, tea, tin	
Somali	91
Cattle, fruit, hides	
Togo	95
Coffee, cotton, copper	
Uganda	71
Copper, coffee, gems	
Zambia	85
Copper, zinc	

Source: *UNCTAD Commodity Yearbook*. New York/Geneva The UN, 1982 (in *Africa Today*: 4th Quarter, 1990:18). Used by permission of *Africa Today*.

Commenting on the African share in the International market, Jennifer Whitaker, who has written extensively on Southern Africa and U.S. policy observes that Africa's traditional sources of revenues have lagged. In countries like Kenya and Cote d'Ivoire coffee and tea flourished and brought occasional windfalls. Unfortunately, many African crops faced greater competition from Asia and Latin America as nations in these regions improved the same crops failing in Africa. This led to an increase in market share in the International trade while African share dropped from 3 percent in 1960 to only 1 percent in 1985. In 1986, Africa's terms of trade plunged an astronomical 29 percent, the region experienced its largest drop in export revenues ever -- from $60 billion to about $44 billion (1988:18).

Export cropping forces small producers and herders onto marginal land, increasing pressure on the environment. Grain yields (per acre) declined by one-third during the past decade due to the shrinking availability of fertile land. The overgrazing and monocropping characteristics of export agriculture have led to the loss of cultivable land to desert and the creation of a hungry, landless underclass that has no alternative but to migrate to the cities. The rise of export cropping in Africa has been accompanied by an increasing dependence on imported food. African wheat imports rose by 250% from 1969 to 1982, just prior to the outbreak of the last famine in Africa. The increase in food imports is more of a reflection of world market forces than of any inherent weakness in African agriculture. Western countries have sought out new markets for the huge grain surpluses they have amassed, driving down prices in the process. The gluts have driven thousands of small grain farmers out of business in Africa, just as in the United States. In both cases, smaller producers simply cannot compete with the major firms of modern corporate businesses.

Declining prices of agricultural commodities have put a further squeeze on many African countries. Unable to change crops or to switch to industrial production, they have simply increased the volume of production, often adding to the downward price spiral. African producers have no influence on the price of these commodities. The United States controls the world price for corn, soybeans, wheat, and rice, due to the sheer volume of its exports. Similarly, Europe sets the world market price for dairy products. In 1985 for instance, the Reagan administration pushed rice prices down by over 50% and corn prices by over 25% to increase U.S. exports. The decline in these prices wrought havoc across Africa and other third world regions. African states have become share croppers on an international scale. They are forced to grow crops they cannot consume or use in order to pay ever expanding debts. In good years they can either keep their agricultural surplus or sell it to buy food. In bad years they cannot survive without help. Even now, one out of every six Africans depends on food aid.

Trying to trace and examine whether the source of the poor economy is based on agriculture, Arnold Rivkin observes that most of the present economic structures are dominated greatly by primary production of agricultural and mineral products as a source of exports, a process developed during the colonial era. The effect has been the exclusion of rational cash crop and industrial production for local markets. The countries use any returns from the exports for financial imports, national development plans, and promotions of private sectors. This has leads to unnecessary use of foreign exchange earned to import domestic products like food stuff to feed the rapidly growing urban population. Money which could be used logically to finance, provide and establish internal industrialization is diverted to other uses (in Paden at el. 1970: 498-499), an objective which needs to be re-evaluated.

The uncertainty as to the best economic system to adopt has been a dominant epidemic in many countries in Africa. Upon independence, many were left unprepared for the system or systems that would suit them.

Many states decided to adopt the colonizers' systems of governments and management while others applied new systems. Not knowing the depth, value or principles involved in these systems, several countries kept on switching from one system to another. Of course, the former colonizers have taken advantage of such unstable behavior by making sure Africa has no strong voice in the world economic trade system. As most countries wondered as to which economic method to adopt, there was confusion among the many alternatives that included: free economy or controlled economy, free market or communism, democratic or socialism, terms that are poorly or narrowly defined. Some countries like Tanzania and Zimbabwe decided to start their own systems based on African ideology and values.

One key element is evident among African states, however. Although torn apart between the best economic system to employ, governments assumed more control over national resources, giving limited power to individuals. In his view, Rivkin feels that the states have "tended to assign a major role in economy building to the government" that has in turn minimized both private entrepreneurs and independent institutions' role. This trend can be explained by lack of capital among private individuals. This would give them the ability and power to establish themselves. The trend can also be associated with lack of cultural traditions necessary "to economic activity involving production for the market." Likewise, the behavior can be related to the psychological compulsion of the countries to match with the modern affluent states and desire to allocate scarce resources with much concern (p.500).

The confusion over the best economic approach to adopt in Africa has not favored a stable economy in the African countries. According to Crawford Young, an Associate Professor of Political Science at the University of Wisconsin, and author of *Politics in Congo* and co-author of *Issues of Political Development,* state-dominated economies and large public sectors have been associated with "oligarchic" or authorization one-party systems. In this kind of environment, there seems to be total contradiction on the part of the state. The states control and centralize all political powers while they still encourage and sanction the "development of independent economic power outside the single, comprehensive political party" (p.501). This trend has not spared individual enterprises and sometimes they have been frustrated in their effort to break away from the systems or when they seem to be having much power. Foreign investors have fled some states in protest over governments' actions while local investors are left to bear the burden of   unstable situations,   and   often become victims of exploitation by their own governments.

Evaluating the African economic performance, the International Bank for Reconstructing and Development, "World Bank and IDA Annual Report 1966/67, reported that:

> During the first half of the Decade of Development -- 1960 - 1965 - the average rate of growth per capital real gross domestic product in Africa was among the lowest in the world, 1.4 percent per annum. This compares with the average rates of growth for all underdeveloped countries of 2.3 percent per annum. It also compares unfavorably with the average rate of growth of 2 percent per annum for the period 1950-55. Thus, Africa since its first decade of independence has been experiencing a decline in the average rate of growth of annual GDP, from 3.9 percent in 1960-65 (1967:26).

The trend of poor performance was not confined only to the 1950s and the 1960s, but continued to the 1980s. In his article entitled, *The O.A.U and The Quest For The Ever elusive Goal of Economic Development*, appearing in *Africa Today,* Ku-Ntima Makidi, observes that serious regional differences were the characteristic of the economic conjuncture in the 1985 period. As a result, when compared to Asia and Latin America, Africa countries performed poorly. It was a surprise that at this period, the oil producing countries which were expected to do   better did worse than non-oil exporters. The slow growth was attributed to slow growth of the U.S. economy, weakness of Africa's trade partners and increase in the deficit of the balance of payment of most countries in Africa (1988:39-40).

With the current situation and trend in the economic crisis, what are the Africans doing? Are they sitting idle to see the continent   head into doom? The answers are examined in the next section.

AFRICAN   GOVERNMENTS'   REACTION   TO ECONOMIC CRISIS

Contrary to negative accusation that Africans   are lazy, less committed and insensitive to African economic problems, African states have been on the forefront to save the   continent's declining economic strength. The efforts have not   been only on African continent   but   reformation of the whole economic system at the global level. Analyzing the African response to the economic crisis, Douglas Lister is extensively   accredited   in this section.   In his support of the positive role by African states, Lister noted that in two main meetings in 1968,   United Nations Conference of Trade and Development   (UNCTAD) in New Delhi and other forums,   the African countries complained vigorously over a system considered to be of generalized preference for the finished and semi-finished goods and services of the rich nations (in Knight 1976:453). How successful the states' efforts are, both locally and at the global level, is an issue of great concern.

Since the UN Special Session in 1987, African states have taken crucial first step to reorder their internal priorities and reorganize their economies. Price controls on some food crops are being loosened to encourage production.

In the face of world economy, Africa's efforts have been frustrated. Being a minority shareholders of the major bodies like   the International Monetary Funds (I.M.F) and the World Bank, the African governments have been forced to turn to regional arrangements in finding solutions to trade and aid crisis. As a result, two forms of arrangement have evolved. These are "vertical" links and "horizontal" links with other African states (Knight   et. el. 1976:448).

Vertical Links

In Africa, vertical links concern monetary ties. For example, virtually all French speaking countries, for instance, Zaire, Congo and Republic of Central Africa, fall under what is called Franc Zone, a zone administered from Paris. Similarly, the association between the European Economic Common Market (EEC)   and the Associated African States and Madagascar (AASM), are vertical in nature. The goal of the European Market is to offer market for African primary products. There is also the goal of financial and technical assistance through the European Development Fund (EDF) and European Investment Bank (EIB). Through this association, there is a joint institution involving both African and European members. The two groups meet periodically to discuss and evaluate the development of commercial preference systems and development aid programs. Through the system, African states are expected to benefit from stable markets for agricultural products without interfering with the system thus making it ineffective. The unreliable factors like drought and famine make the African countries unable to supply stable or fixed inputs into the market. Another important factor for both French-zone and ECC, is that they are external bodies rather than African bodies. This brings up the point raised earlier where the African countries have less control of the decisions made. The states' participation in meeting is vital but without much contribution in the market, they do not benefit greatly.

Horizontal Links

Unlike vertical links that are externally managed and monitored, horizontal links are internal, existing in every sub region of the continent. It is a system that reflects traditional trade in the continent.

In East Africa, horizontal links started as early as the turn of the Century when both Kenya and Uganda formed a Custom Union. This was followed by the formation of the East African Community (E.A.C.) which included Kenya, Uganda and Tanzania, the three predominant East African countries. The purpose of the E.A.C. was to allow its members observe a common external tariff, trade within the community without restriction, and harmonize internal policies especially those concerning industrial development. But like any other organizations in the continent, E.A.C. faced several problems. Its effort to distribute industries among members gave rise to severe rivalry. Political animosity also greatly interfered with the running of the organization. As a result of internal conflicts, the E.A.C. collapsed in 1977. This left the countries involved frustrated and blaming each other.

Like East Africa, Central African countries have an economic organization known as Union Dovaniere et Economique De I'Afrique Central (U.D.E.A.C.). Like the Custom Union that pioneered the East Africa Community, the U.D.E.A.C was pioneered by Union Dovaniere Equatoriale (U.D.E) with its existence and operation beginning during the colonial era. With the goal of promoting a stable economy, U.D.E.A.C. compensates poor members for losses that they may incur in the integration process. By 1976, the organization included Central African Republic, Congo, Gabon and Cameroon.

Unlike both East and Central Africa where only one major body exists, there are three economic bodies in West Africa. The first is the Conseil De L'Entente that is composed of Dahomey, Niger, Upper Volt, Ivory Coast (Cote d'Ivoire) and Togo. It is a political organization that has created mutual aid and loan guarantee fund. The purpose of the fund program is to provide and guarantee loans to individual members using the group's resources. The second group is the Union Dovanie're De L'Afrique De L'Ouest (UDAO) which is only a custom union. This ensures a common external tariff for members while they trade amongst themselves in a relatively free environment. By 1976, members of UDAO included Ivory Coast, Niger, Upper Volta, Mauritania, Senegal, Dahomey and Mali. The third group was formed in 1975 at Lagos, Nigeria. The 15 West African nations from both Anglo and Francophone agreed to create the Economic Community of West Africa (ECOWA), with a goal of bringing positive impact on development, spatial organization and interaction of members of the region (pp. 452-453).

Another major body is the Lake Chad Basin Commission participating both English and French speaking countries. Its members are Chad, Cameroon, Niger and Nigeria. The goal is to promote economic relationship among members.

In East and Central Africa, member states have also established another economic body known as the Preferential Trade Association (P.T.A.) The objective of the body is to ensure regional growth by encouraging trade between members. It is also the aim of the organization to control external tariffs while ensuring relative restrictions between members. Some members are Zimbabwe, Zambia, Uganda, Tanzania, and Kenya. The body hopes to include more states as it matures.

How effective are these horizontal links? Though started with the aim of regional economical promotions and growth, the different bodies are faced by almost common problems. Some of the problems encountered are regional balance of payment deterioration that becomes worse each year. Another reason for declining trade surplus is an increasing demand for import. In most of the African countries, development has been matched with larger amounts of transport and manufactured goods. This leads to increase in demand for spare parts, technicians, and consultants. As development grows, people enlarge their demand for foreign goods while they lower demand for local manufactured goods and services.

Also, with fluctuating market condition of African agricultural products and minerals, the terms of trade have been less favorable to Africa. The states' efforts to stabilize the economy are always faced with undesirable effect. Without the technical capability required, Africa continues to lag behind, a process that may persist unless brought under control.

AFRICA AND THE FUTURE CHALLENGES

Does the African continent have any future or is it doomed to failure? This is a key question considering the fact that nearly all methods employed to bring economic prosperity are faced with frustrations and discouragement. Faced with this situation, clearly the continent is experiencing a tough time. The present situation cannot be rectified by blaming each other or blaming the Western nations. The fact that Africa holds a small share of the world economy means the continent has to establish its economic stability by focusing more closely on the internal strategies, strengthen its policy and bargaining power in the face of the world.

The burgeoning debt, Western trade policies, and war constitute major and so far almost overwhelming obstacles to self sustaining development. Although the African states have called for conversion of their debt to a mix of grants and long-term, low-interest loans with a ten year grace period before payments are due, few Western creditors are really willing to actually write off the loans. The Western creditors have however been willing to reschedule debts to avoid default. Movement on issues like the debt will take far-reaching policy changes in the industrial countries that profit from Africa's misery. These changes are not likely to occur without informed and sustained public pressure. Political organization in industrial countries should focus on pressuring Western governments and banks to cancel much of their African debt. Even with a write down of debt, it will be difficult for the African economies to recover until interest rates, exchange rates, and world commodity prices are stabilized. North-South international negotiations should focus on lessening the price disparity between goods produced by third world nations-agricultural commodities and raw materials -- and the manufactured goods of the industrial countries. Addressing such inequities might mean that the U.S. consumers for instance would pay more for their coffee and cocoa but the pay back is potentially greater. The stability of the international economy would increase and international tensions would subside.

The importance of strong internal economical ties for African states cannot be emphasized enough. Only when the continent has been put in proper order will its policies be sound. Only when a stronghold has been attained will the continent win challenges in the face of the world. It would then stand a chance of being successful. For such a success to be attained, there needs to be a keen sense of political stability, proper management, trust and commitment on the part of leadership of these countries. This would lead to a healthy relationship among and between nations of Africa. A relationship that will lead to a strong voice on the world economy and trade. Supporting the view of economic integration among the African states as a real concern for the states, Salim Ahmed Salim, the Organization of African Union (O.A.U.) Secretary General notes that:

> The fact that now people are talking in terms of taking the question on integration seriously, the fact that our leaders and our governments are now addressing themselves to the question of conflict resolutions and conflict management -- these are indicative of the significance that we attach to the question of change in our continent . . . . (*African Report*, May June 1992:39).

The Secretary General's conclusion on what the African states are doing to rectify their already devastated economic situation, is necessary and the countries are challenged to make this practical.

There is a need for unity among the countries because, the roots of financial crisis have been put on the colonial master of the continent. It is not time to focus on such past remedies. It is time to focus on the future, a bright future. It should be clear among the states that the world economy has not favored the continent. While prices of most African agricultural and mineral commodities exported continued to face poor pricing over the last three decades, the states should not expect a change in trend. If anything, the condition is expected to get worse.

Relying on the foreign nations to assist the continent is necessary but the continent should use such assistance to realize her common goal, rather than for selfish gain or for promoting internal conflict. It is not conflict, war, or accusation that would solve African economic problems. It is the unity of the continental states to achieve a common goal -- development. As Karamo Sonko notes:

Our world is no longer the world of our forefathers, not even the world
that existed in the aftermath of World War II. Instead, we live in a highly
interconnected and interdependent world that functions as a mechanical
rather than an organic whole. A malfunctioning in each component affects
and sends vital currents throughout the system, as vibrations in any unit
would stimulate activity in the rusty part. No longer can we afford to think
of maintaining global community in which a small section thrives while
the rest dies. Issues of poverty, human rights and democracy,
desertification and deforestation are now transcending ideological and
national frontiers into the global realm. We have almost reached a stage
where all nations either swim together or sink together. This is not simply
a moralistic or sentimental plea. In the area of international trade, for
instance, statistical data and econometric studies or repercussion effects
and income multipliers have become the essence of international policy
debates . . . Political and environmental linkages create an even greater
tendency towards a monolithic destiny for all contemporary nations.
Certainly one of the most important issues in the area of international
relations today is that of Third World debt . . . The debt crisis has begun
to serve as the forum and indication of these questions and the imminent
"cold war" between developed and developing/Third World countries.
There is no shortage of solutions to this crisis; the problem is the need for
the will to implement them. Although this is the overriding concern, we
should not lose sight of the fact that even if all the debt is canceled today,
many problems that led to the current crisis will continue to exist.
Therefore, major policy changes in both creditor and debtor nations are
required in order to generate long-term economic prosperity in Africa and
the rest of the developing countries. Thus a buoyant world economy can be
created and the tendency toward intra-national and international conflict
halted. The critical factor is the will to act where there is a need to act.
(*Africa Today* 4th Quarter, 1990:26).

CASE STUDY 4.1

JAPAN AS A MODEL OF DEVELOPMENT FOR DEVELOPING COUNTRIES

WHAT CAN AFRICA LEARN FROM JAPAN? A LOOK AT JAPAN'S RISE AS AN ECONOMIC POWER AND THE COLLABORATIVE RELATIONSHIP BETWEEN JAPANESE BUSINESS, GOVERNMENT, AND SOCIETY.

The biggest success story in Asia and a prime model for countries looking to improve their own economic lot is Japan. In 1952 the U.S. occupation of Japan following World War II ended, and Japanese business and government leaders began to develop and implement policies aimed at promoting national economic growth. These policies centered on providing for increasing investment in the infrastructure and manufacturing capacity of the country and generating resources internally by personal consumption and government expenditures. Investment incentives were specifically targeted in special areas of the economy that utilized the relative advantages of the country.

Japan is severely limited in its physical attributes and has few resources in the form of land, energy sources, or minerals. Thus, development was directed away from agricultural production, which was relatively inefficient and of low value, and toward creating manufacturing capacity. This type of realistic focus led to an increase in Japan's GNP by five times in the period from 1954 to 1971.

Initially, in the 1950s Japan focused on export-led growth as a policy and looked to marketing opportunities in the U.S. market, which had the advantages of size, depth, and openness. In addition to these factors, the cold was between the United States and the Soviet Union served to promote close ties between the United States and Japan, an important ally country close to the Soviet Union's Pacific borders.

After identifying markets with the greater long-term potential, Japanese policymakers looked closely at developing an appropriate group of products to promote for export to new markets and implemented policies to support and promote those specific industries in a timed sequence. At first the nation relied on areas where it already had some expertise and could use its labor advantages. These areas were textile manufacturing and toy production, and although the goods produced were relatively inexpensive, substantial profits were earned from the high sales volumes.

This growth in sales and markets allowed the Japanese focus to shift to higher value-added products, such as cameras, videotape players, watches, computers, printers, and word processors; vehicles, such as cars, trucks, motorcycles, and construction equipment; and capital-intensive goods, such as steel and ocean-going ships.

Japanese Methodology

In order to implement these plans and achieve success, it was necessary for Japan to embody these plans in effective and flexible national policies. The initial need was to generate money to be invested and channeled into the designed growth areas. Japan, therefore, chose a policy of encouraging private savings and investment, avoiding government borrowing from other countries or commercial lenders. The policy obviated the need to attract foreign direct investment and avoided state involvement in industry.

In order to yield sufficient savings to finance such rapid growth, japan implemented a number of incentives for savings and investment by private   citizens. These policies included penalizing consumer borrowing through taxes and promoting savings with tax exemptions for interest income on investments. In addition, the country established a national savings system and placed limits on capital transfer out of the country. The country's citizens also were provided with incentives to save for their future, because the government provided only a rudimentary public welfare system. Thus, taxation and other policies made it only reasonable for the Japanese to invest their funds where they would have the greatest tax-free returns to provide for retirement income. The result was a private savings rate of 28 percent in 1971, which was more than triple the average annual rate of citizens in most developed countries.

The savings system provided industry in Japan with an enormous pool of investment funds and allowed companies to operate and grow without incurring vast amounts of debt. The flow of the funds to appropriate industries and sectors of the economy was facilitated by the operation of the nation's banks and special purpose organizations designed to promote industrial development in the country. Overseeing the operation of these entities were government ministries, primarily the Ministry of Finance and the Bank of Japan. This investment became the driving force in spurring economic development in the 1960s.

These government arms acted in concert with another powerful entity in Japanese economic circles -- the Ministry of International Trade and Industry (MITI). This and other government agencies next looked toward developing a base of technological expertise that could move the economy from being labor intensive to being more capital intensive and make it less volatile and vulnerable. Thus, Japan began acquiring technological skills through a variety of methods, including buying and leasing technology from foreign suppliers; developing its own technological base through research and development; importing technology, by allowing foreign companies to work within the nation in joint ventures; and using reverse engineering to learn about technological developments, that is, buying products that use new technologies and closely observing and analyzing their operation in order to replicate them in home manufacturing facilities.

Japan's industrial base shifted from a reliance on textile and steel production to the export of sophisticated higher-priced and value-added goods, such as cars, ships, televisions, and tape recorders. Textiles, for example, had made up nearly half of Japan's exports in 1950 but comprised only 5 percent by 1985. Exports soared as Japan made the shift from cheap goods to high quality, sophisticated, and technological developed product classes.

At the same time, national policies were designed to emphasize production and exports while limiting imports into the country. The objective of these policies was to maintain a favorable balance of trade, with exports for out balancing imports.

Imports were kept low through the imposition of stiff tariffs and nontariff barriers. Although in recent years Japan has slowly opened its borders to foreign goods, under the pressure of its trading partners, these barriers to imports are still significant, especially for consumer goods. A U.S. journalist based in Japan, described problems in the consumer economy of Japan, noted his 1988 attempt to buy slippers from a mail-order company in the United States for $27 that resulted in his paying import duties of $39 per pair. Such duties effectively prohibit the importation of many summer goods into Japanese markets, and imports are composed mostly of luxury goods, entertainment items, and raw materials.

These policies were implemented as part of comprehensive national industries policy. As U.S. journalist Janus Fallow pointed out, "All parts of this strategy were supported by a pervasive, well-coordinated management of Japanese economic affairs by the elite bureaucracies. Seldom in the modern world, at least in peacetime, had the government of an advanced democratic country instituted such a thorough going system of business incentives within a national economy, and never had such an effort under such conditions proved so phenomenally successful." These policies included not only a framework for the creation on economic growth through the promotion of investment in certain industries, but also provided for divestment in areas in which the country no longer held competitive advantage or preeminence. For these "sunset" industries, the government imposed a method of orderly shutdowns so that declines in specific industries did not lead to vast and extensive disruption in the economy.

The Japanese Way

One notable aspect of the business environment in Japan that differs greatly from most Western or industrialized countries, but which greatly facilities the efficacy on industries plans is the strong association between business and government in working toward mutual goals. This collaboration differs greatly in the United States, where the relationship between business interest and government is often more adversarial than collaborative. In Japan, goals are achieved through harmony, cooperation, and individual sacrifice. The structure of the business world is also more oriented toward collaborative efforts between government and with other businesses than in other nations. For example, in Japan much business is conducted by large groups of companies and banks called keiretus. Within these groups, manufacturing is coordinated among the member companies from the provision of raw materials to the production of intermediate goods, including parts of the overall financing of operations. This is accomplished through communication and coordinated decision-making throughout the network of affiliated businesses, corporations, and banks. It is common in Japan for banks to own stock in individual companies and for directors on the their boards to sit on the boards of manufacturing companies. Such relationships and business activities would quickly run afoul of antitrust laws in countries such as the United States.

In addition to a healthy and productive relationship between government and business in Japan, economic progress and development has been achieved through systematic efforts to provide extensive education for the populace and by thorough training of corporate employees. In addition to sending many students abroad to study at universities that are strong in basic research, the government also sponsors study missions to learn from other countries. It also coordinates extensive research and development efforts or consortia of scientists who work to develop technology for commercial product applications.

Japanese Economic Growth

Growth in the Japanese GNP has far outstripped growth in the U.S. GNP and in the countries of the European Economic Community (EEC). From 1961 to 1965, Japan's growth rate average 10 percent compared to levels closer to 5 percent for both the United States and the EEC. This spread widened to an average 11 percent from 1966 to 1970 for Japan, compared to only 3 percent for the United States and 4.4 percent for the EEC. Even in subsequent years, growth rates in Japan almost always exceeded those of other industrialized nations.

Japan's growth slowed in the 1970s, primarily because of the shocks experienced around the world because of rapid and severe increase in the prices of oil. These increase had a profound effect upon Japan, because the country had to import large amounts of fuel, particularly oil, which account for 90 percent of all its energy imports in 1973. The price jump led to serious problems in Japan in the 1970s -- high inflation, a large balance-of-payments deficit, and the most severe recession since World War II. In addition, the country was also experiencing inflation because of continued stimulation of the economy by the government to maintain high levels of growth. In response to the economic problems existing in the country in 1974, the government tightened the money supply considerably to eliminate inflation and allowed higher prices for energy to flow through to consumer pocketbooks in the form of higher prices for consumer goods.

These increased costs created a major impetus to conserve energy in Japan and, consequently, spurred the development of new fuel-efficient technologies and more productive manufacturing practices to reduce Japanese dependence on expensive foreign oil and to cut labor and other production costs. Efforts toward developing greater efficiencies were conducted in tandem with organized industry reductions of excess capacity. In order to achieve capacity reductions, representatives of industry and government officials joined together to decide how to equitably reduce capacity within industry. The objective of these actions and policies was to raise productivity, lower labor costs, and reallocate labor to more productive areas, so that the efficient use of labor and energy would yield advantages to producers in the form of lower product costs and result in increased competitiveness for Japanese goods. Consequently, Japanese labor productivity increased by one-fifth between 1974 and 1980.

This movement was accomplished by the continuing shift in production emphasis from low-value to high-value products, such as

Electronic equipment and automobiles. In addition, production techniques began to rely more heavily on the use of industrial robots for repetitive processes.

In the late 1970s, service industries expanded rapidly, while there were continued reductions in oil use and increases in exports. In 1984 exports comprised 17 percent of the Japanese GNP, as compared to 9 percent of its GNP in the 1960s.

Present-Day Japan

Throughout the 1980s, Japan has continued its shift to higher-value products and out of industries where it no longer holds a competitive edge in World markets, such as in shipbuilding and textile manufacturing. The current emphasis is on industries driven by high technology, such as consumer electronics, computers, and sophisticated technical equipment. After the recession of 1985, the country once again began a program of adjustment, which includes the contracting of extra production and labor capacity and the redirection of investment to new plants to reduce costs of production and maintain product competitiveness. The biggest difference between this adjustment and those of prior years is that Japan is now using a great deal of offshore production, where it formerly relied solely on efficiencies, to be gained in domestic manufacturing. Thus Japanese companies are expanding horizontally, but into other nations of east Asia, where labor costs are cheaper that at home.

Years of continued economic progress and trade surpluses have enabled Japan to build important competitive strengths. Partly because of its drive for production efficiency and conservation and partly because of the structural shift in Japanese industry, its dependence on raw material imports has fallen dramatically. In fact, Japan is less dependent on imported raw materials than Great Britain, France, West German, or Italy.

Substantial overseas investments during the years of consistent trade surpluses have began to yield dividends. Income from "invisible" (such as services) is beginning to exceed expenditures, which will add another major strength to Japan's balance of payments position and would serve as a stabilizer even in the unlikely situation that Japan faces a trade deficit in a particular year.

Source: Reprinted with the permission of Prentice Hall, Inc. from *International Business: Theory and Practice.* By Riad A. Ajami and Dara Khambata. Copyright 1992 by Macmillan College Publishing Company.

Questions

1.   Why should Japan decide to trade with a country that occupied it following the end of World War II?

2. What strategy did Japanese have in order to penetrate the huge American market? Do you think Africa can use such a strategy to expand its market abroad? Explain.

3. Why do you think Japan has continued to resist its partners' pressure to open its local market especially on consumer products? Do you think this is helpful to Japan?

4. How effective was Japan's method of restricting borrowing from abroad while encouraging local savings and investments?

5. Describe Japan's Government's relationship with business communities. Is it possible for African governments to establish such relationships?

6. Which industries are described as "sunset" industries and why did the Government decide to shut them?

7. Describe Japan's road to development since 1952 and before 1960.

8. Describe Africa's road to development since 1960.

9. What have you learnt about development in particular?

10. "Africa has numerous resources as compared to Japan and should be able to stand by itself." Discuss this statement.

11. What is Japan's future as a world economic leader?

12. What is Africa's future as a world's poorest continent? Can the destiny be altered? Explain.

Chapter Five

MANAGEMENT: ARE AFRICAN POOR MANAGERS?

Management has been defined as the ability to plan, direct, coordinate, forecast and organize. Effective management is achieved when the set goals and objectives are successfully fulfilled. This means that resources are well coordinated and employed. Management effectiveness is especially necessary, considering the fact that resources are scarce. We cannot emphasis enough the need for good management if we have to be good stewards of our environment and society.

Good planning and forecasting facilitate the stewardship of scarce resources. Economists have classified resources into four parts: land, capital, labor, and technology. These four, also known as factors of production, determine the level of choice and the required combinations in order to achieve equitable resources allocation. According to economists, the ability to combine the four factors is known as substitutability. The factors complement each other to a certain degree depending on the demand and desired output. Through proper organization and implementation, then cost-effectiveness is achieved thereby leading to maximum output. It is the goal of any sector of the economy to maximize output while minimizing cost, unless otherwise stated. While the whole process of achieving good output or return is complex, it is clear that proper management is a prerequisite for success.

Unlike economists who classify resources in terms of labor, capital, land, and technology, management schools of thought view resources in five different forms, often referred to as the Five Ms (5Ms). That is, management resources are men, money, machines, methodology, and market. The 5Ms have to coordinate well if organizations or firms are to be effective and productive. Apart from man who is static, all other resources are flexible. This means that while the other four resources can be manipulated and shaped in accordance to the desired effect, man has to be treated differently. Management scholars feel that a manager has first to learn how to manage his fellow men who in turn will manage other resources.

The emphasis on man is   key   in the management process. Management can be said to   refer to man. To illustrate this point further, the word MANAGEMENT is a derivative of men; that is "manage", and "men". Note also that the word MANAGEMENT has man in   the first three letters. This leads us to the phrase "man - manage - men." The conclusion is important when considering that the term "man" in Management comes from a Latin word   that is literary interpreted to mean directing, controlling, and the ability to hold the control of people.   It is through the ability to have man well managed that the scarce resources can be well maintained.

But management is not an easy task. Practitioners have tried to develop theories aimed at understanding man and how to make him more manageable. To some practitioners, management is a jungle where no one approach   can be accepted as the best.   Other see management as a science   and others as an art.   However, the practitioners are responsible for developing principles necessary to manage   resources. The   social science approach has viewed management as an art subject because it cannot be tested in a laboratory. This has led to research   geared to find a more acceptable approach to management. The   final   conclusion   being   that management is the art and science of getting   things done through people. Management is a science due to the methods used to develop principles. Similarly, it is   an art due to the application of the principles developed. The greatest problem facing man is not how to manage land, capital and technology -- factors of production --- the problem is the management of his fellow man (labor).

ARE   AFRICANS   POOR   MANAGERS   OF RESOURCES?

The question as to whether Africans are   poor managers of resources has become critical in recent years. On the basis of the above discussion, to be a poor manager of resources means to have inadequate knowledge of how to manage effectively, or misusing resources. It also means that people are not well managed, negating the effective management of resources: - capital, land, and technology -- as economists would term them or -- money, machines, market and technology -- as management practitioners would refer to production and management of resources. As a result, resources are poorly allocated.

This chapter aims at exploring whether the accusation is true or not and what can be done to solve any management crisis if any. Several questions form the basis of my argument. Is it true that Africans are poor managers, or is this another propaganda from the West used to blame Africans? Who is to blame if true or false? Is there a solutions to the accusation? And how long will it take before a a clear understanding of the issue is achieved?

The Quality of Management in Africa

The quality of management in Africa can be measured by a proper evaluation of the way institutions are performing. Both public and private, governments and non-government institutions. A good analysis will show that even those projects started by the Europeans during colonial era are falling apart (See the case study). While Africans have accused foreign powers of interfering with the management of institutions, the Europeans have blamed African leaders as being inadequate and having conflicts of interest. In its evaluation of over a thousand projects started in the 1970s, the World Bank report of 1985, indicated that project, programs and policies failed to meet the set objectives. In comparing Africa's performance with other world developing countries, the report showed that the developing countries' project failure averaged 12 percent. The projects, either failed to achieve their objectives or led to an uncertain outcome. When compared to two sub-Sahara regions, the result of performance was quite alarming. In West Africa, projects failed at the rate of 18 percent while in East Africa, the rate was 24 percent. A focus on specific projects indicated that almost one agricultural project out of three failed in West Africa and half failed in East Africa. This is surprising when compared to South Asian countries where only one project failed out of twenty started (Harrison 1987:48). This indicates a wide range of problems with project performance from West Africa across to the East Africa. The World Bank evaluation has shown that most African projects are usually successful in their early years but often fail as soon as the donors have withdrawn. It is possible that other areas of development could be failing at an even high rate (p.48). Projects failure are widely spread in Africa and one is left with the question: Why does Africa lead in this embarrassing field and what could be associated with such projects and other development failure?

One answer lies in political crisis in most countries. In Africa, the deciding factors for decisions are political giants who oversee all spheres of a country's development. With power struggle and desires, most of the decisions are made by "giants", often politicians, with the goal of benefiting themselves. Millions of dollars which have been siphoned to foreign banks though meant to develop the countries. This money, once banked outside, becomes the property of those concerned rather than for assisting the projects and people. One approach to solve the problem is have the forgers resign from governments. Unfortunately, this does not mean that they give up the money they have taken to foreign banks. It is like telling them that it is time to go to use stolen money without the interference of the governments.

Looking at the whole process of projects' development and failure, it can be said that the problem is not solely that of management. This is especially true considering that such projects are successful when started. Several other factors are associated with failure.

Greed associated with corruption may be a key cause of failure. This can be seen when considering the fact that many people employed to run projects are well trained and highly educated. It is unfortunate that many run the project with a fixed desire to benefit self rather than the community. Let me explain this point further.

Culture Of Eating

One thing that has overtaken people in Africa and other developing countries is what journalists have termed as "the culture of eating." By this concept, a certain percent of a project's budgets goes to bribing the authorities, or other leaders required to have a budget approved. Many European countries have complained of many incidents where they find themselves confronted by demand for bribery. While some have submitted to the demands, some have informed their governments which in turn have withdrawn their aid or assistance to projects. Let me also mention that some foreign corporations have been accused of offering bribes in order to acquire contracts or markets in Africa.

People in leadership and management offices, whether government or non-government, banks, or other institutions have developed the mentality of "eating". In governments, for example, appointments or promotions seem to indicate who will eat next and how much. The behavior shows how selfish some people can be. Unless such beliefs are totally churned out from the society, the problem of resource misuse and mismanagement will prevail for a long time. When there is a feeling of responsibility and accountability, then a country wins leading to achievement of a higher level of management and development.

Being greedy has hindered development of the continent's economy and promoted self-gain leading to national economic failure. The attitude and belief that "I need to eat as much as possible because tomorrow I might not be there" has led to a vicious cycle which has continued to kill institutions and society moral. Instead of focusing on growth, development, efficiency, and technological management, projects, churches, banks and governments are falling apart. And dissatisfied with the results, the mass population in many countries have responded by rising against their governments or projects' heads. For organizations which may fail, for example, banks and public institutions, the governments may react by putting them under receivership. This was true in Kenya in the 1980s and early 1990s when several financial institutions faced financial crisis and the public fund was at risk. Responding to public cries, the government placed many of the financially troubled institutions under receivership to ensure public funds safety. This move helped many people who could have lost much money trusted in the institutions.

Public bodies have also been victims of poor management as leaders consume funds meant to run them. To ensure their declining production is controlled, the government of Kenya opened several of them to the public to buy shares and ownership through privatization. The move aims at generating more accountability and responsibility among those concerned. In Tanzania, the move hopes to improve the production in many sectors as individuals become more committed to their businesses than those run by the government. This goal is realized considering the fact that citizens should be productive and must work toward the expansion and growth of their economy. The result is an increase in production, self-sustained economy which sustains the rest of the population. Africa needs to focus in this direction, a concept not well facilitated today.

Inadequate Training

From the on going argument, it may appear as if, greed which promotes the culture of eating is the only cause of poor management. However, poor training has a major role to play in the whole sector of development. Many leaders holding high positions and management officers are poorly trained and equipped for jobs or duties they perform. There are many coups and counter coup experienced in many African countries. The new leaders have given many poorly trained personnel responsibilities that demand high training and experience. While some have received military training and basic education , others get management placement through nepotism. And without the required skills, many run their economies like grocery stores or restaurants.

Most managers and top executives, both in African and outside, feel that consulting their juniors in matters of importance is stooping too low. They trust their consciousness and cultural beliefs which may mislead them at times. Many take decisions and enforce implementation without involving professionals in particular fields. For example, a professional who is younger than a manager could be ignored when decisions requiring his or her inputs are made. This often leads to line-staff conflict and generation gaps become obvious. The problem is enforced by African culture where senior members of the society see young people as inexperienced and requiring advise and direction irrespective of their age. There is an African saying that "when children learn to wash their hands, they can eat with elders." This shows how young people are regarded in families, a concept which is easily transferred to both governments and development programs. The effect is conflict with the management principle of a two-way communication. With poor communication, the organizational atmosphere is endangered, goals are unclear, conflict of interest arises, resistance among groups results, all affecting productivity of the corporations or projects. In many countries, reasonable moves to rectify and correct those in authority is often met with violence. In the political arena, those who speak against a given decision taken by the governments are seen as political opposition advocates and are suppressed.   They may be detained, harassed, victimized, abused or exiled. Many examples exist, especially with the call for multi-party governments in an effort to establish "democracy" in Africa (see Chapter Three on democracy). However, it should not be thought that only Africa has this type of problem. The United States where democracy and level of education is high has also experienced similar problems.

Nepotism and Management

Is management affected by nepotism? The question needs careful analysis because the Western world finds it hard to accept nepotism as a remedy to development. Being an individualistic society, Western country members operate independently and individually. An individual behavior or act is rarely influenced by parents, or relatives. Once mature, the person is expected to start, monitor, and manage his or her own life. As a result, there is little dependence on each other. This evaluation is not an assessment of good or bad, but merely stress the contrast between Western life style and African life styles. Even in the West, nepotism has its room and has existed.

In Africa, an individual is part of the community. An individual decision is considered in terms of societal gains or loss. An African man is part of his community irrespective of what he thinks. He may disown his people but that will not deny the fact that he is part of an extended family and ancestors. He is expected to care and protect the society and all its virtues. In a family circle, he is not only responsible for his nuclear family, but also his extended family. Whether in school, church, work or visiting, he is expected to think about his family members, and find ways of assisting them. The African saying that "I am because you are," shows the deep cultured relationship that the person exists because of the community or society in which he has grown. What may be termed as nepotism by others will be viewed as an expectation by those involved.

The African concept of nepotism closely ties with the original usage of the term. Nepotism has its root in French and Latin, "Nipote" French for nephew or "Nepos", Latin for grandson. It shows a blood relationship or very close relationship, just as those involved often had close contact. The meaning differs slightly from the dictionary term which denotes favoritism shown to a relative. Both meanings can apply to both western and western worlds, Africa and non-Africa, white or non-whites nepotism is seen as giving appointment to relatives because of their due placements in the family rather than on merits: education, professionals, or experience.

Since time immemorial, Africans have used nepotism as a virtue rather than a favor. Chief and kings choose those they want in their families or ethnic groups. It was a process of enhancing trust, strength, and royalty in the societies. It was and still is a form of improving the family status in the societies. For example, if a relative was poor, another relative may give a cow in the hope that the beneficially will improve his or her living standard.

Management Solutions

Political crisis, greed, lack of adequate training, and nepotism are some of the factors which have been associated with poor management of resources in Africa. Africa, like many other continents, cannot expect to survive in the future if the prevailing behavior continue to exist. A solution is required which will see to it that management is well facilitated to the satisfaction of the public equity. The belief that "I need to make use of what is there today because I might not be there tomorrow" shows lack of concern and being short-sighted. You may not be there but your children or gland children will. You may not be there to see the suffering of your children but that does not mean they will not suffer. Solving the current problem means preparing Africa to be a better place for the future generations. The fact that one has suffered does not mean everyone should suffer. Being patriotic means acting with concern and care for one's country. Many people died fighting for the independent of their countries so that the future will bring brightness for all. Like Nelson Mandela, the President of South Africa has said, "South Africa's future depends on the cooperation of all races and ethnic groups."

Promotion of one group does not ensure development, but suffering of the unfavored group -- a concept which was well demonstrated by the white rule during apartheid period.

Africa's management of resources calls for love of the continent and being long sighted about the future. It requires working together and pulling all resources in a more loving way. It means coordinating all factors of production in the most efficient way to facilitate development. It means using the available resources in the most productive way. Resources are rare and need to be managed as so. The quality of African management lies with the Africans -- failure or success. As Africans, let us be responsible, accountable, self-giving, committed and loving, both to mankind and the environment. We can achieve this through proper management of our resources.

CASE STUDY 4.1

DEVELOPING AFRICA[1]

AFRICAN DEVELOPMENT REMAINS A CHALLENGE AND A MAJOR CONCERN
TO THE WORLD. IN THEIR STRIVE TO DEVELOP, MANY AFRICAN
COUNTRIES HAVE SUFFERED. MANY HAVE TAKEN THE WRONG DIRECTION
AND IT HAS BEEN DIFFICULT FOR SOME TO COME BACK TO THE RIGHT
DIRECTION. DIRECTIVES FROM THOSE WHO ADVOCATE DIFFERENT
PHILOSOPHIES FOR THE CONTINENT HAVE NOT HELPED AFRICA AND IN
MANY INSTANCES HAVE LED TO DEVASTATING RESULTS. THIS HAS
EMPHASIZED THE FACT THAT AFRICAN CRISIS ARE DEEP ROOTED THAN
MOST ADVOCATES COMPREHEND. THE PRESENT CASE AIMS AT
EXPLORING TWO PROJECTS AND HOW THEY WERE MANAGED AND WHAT
LED TO THEIR FAILURE. IT WAS PREPARED BY R. L. STIRRAT, A SENIOR
LECTURER IN SOCIAL ANTHROPOLOGY IN THE SCHOOL OF AFRICAN AND
ASIAN STUDIES, UNIVERSITY OF SUSSEX.

ONE ASPECT OF the growth of the development industry, reckoned
in 1989 to be worth around US $56 billion per annum, [2] has been the
emergence of the 'aid community', people whose lives depend on the
continuation of the development industry in something like its present
form. In part composed of permanent employees, the majority are
employed on fixed term contracts either as 'Associate Professional
Officers', 'Technical Cooperation Officers' or whatever, or as short
term consultants. Members of this community shift from one donor
agency to another and their careers resemble the 'spiralists' of 1960s'
sociology, moving around the world from one consultancy to the next
or from one longer term posting to another with occasional sojourns in
the capitals of the development industry such as Rome, Washington
and New York.

Just as the colonial rulers of the past created the object of their rule,
so too does the developing industry. In the past, the colonial
authorities spent what might seem an inordinate amount of time and
effort systematizing their knowledge of the societies which they ruled,
and in the process frequently created what it was that they ruled. In
India this involved the regularization and systematization of the
system of castes and religious groupings, a 'freezing' of history as
means of creating a governable state.[3] Similarly, in Africa, ethnic
identity was regularized and manipulated to invent or at least rigidify
tribal boundaries and divisions.[4] As Adam Ashforth puts it in his
discussion of Commissions of Inquiry in twentieth century South
Africa, government reports, 'contract[ed] authoritative understandings

of social reality which provide 'scientific' grounds for treating 'society' as if constituted as a material thing with a single constitutive logic'(p.254)[5]. Similarly, the development industry creates its own object of work, a necessity in a world in which short term consultants may only be in a country for a few weeks, and flitting from one continent to another with remarkable speed. In part this involves the use of a general model of what underdevelopment is; in part it involves the generation of particular views of particular countries, all aspects of the construction of a particular discourse, 'devspeak'.

James Ferguson's The Anti-Politics Machines is an anthropological study of one development project in central Lesotho. This project, mainly funded by Canada, ran from 1975 to 1984, and was concerned at various times with livestock development, agricultural improvement and administrative change. However, Ferguson is not concerned with the project's failure per se. Rather, he approaches the project itself as an object of study and attempts to understand the logic of the project in terms of the manner in which the development industry works and the particular discourse it employs.

The first chapters deal at length with delineating the development discourse of the aid community. For Ferguson, to ask whether or not the development industry is a 'good thing' or a 'bad thing' or whether aid program's help the poor are naive questions. Rather, if we want to understand 'development' and the 'development industry' we have to examine the apparatus that purports to do the developing.

Furthermore, we have to move beyond a narrow focus on 'objective interests' and begin to see institutions and discourses as the proper foci of attention. Drawing largely on Foucault, Fergurson argues that the intentions of development planners bear an extremely problematic relationship to the outcomes of their planning.[6] Intentional plans are always important but never in quite the way the planners imagined' (p.20)

Given the pressures of consultancy work, it is not surprising that many consultants and other development personnel depend on the products of the wealthiest and most powerful institution in the development industry: the World Bank. In particular, the 'Country Reports' produced by the Bank are frequently used by other donors without any critical appraisal, the argument being that other donors cannot hope to rival the expertise of the Bank and should not waste time and resources on their own studies. Ferguson begins his study with a detailed analysis of the 1975 Country Report on Lesotho with the aim of understanding the 'discursive framework' of the report and why such reports have to be written and constructed as the are.

In a fascinating analysis Ferguson shows that the representation of

Lesotho in the report is almost unrecognizable to anyone who knows the country. Rather than acknowledge that Lesotho has been part of the market economy since the nineteenth century and that it has depended on migrant labor to South African mines for a similar length of time, the report attempts to define the country as a 'traditional substance peasant society', virtually untouched by modern economic development'. More generally in the sort of development discourse epitomized by the report, Lesotho becomes 'a nation of farmers, not wage laborers; a country with a geography, but no history; with people, but no classes; values, but no structures; administrators, but no rulers; bureaucrats, but no politics' (p.66).

For Ferguson, the important point is not that the Bank's picture of Lesotho is wrong but that it is systematically wrong compared with the academic discourse which deals with Lesotho. 'The statistics are wrong, but always in the same way; the conceptions are fanciful, but it is always the same fantasy . . . [A]ll "development" discourse on Lesotho seems to tend towards the picture of Lesotho as a species of a well known genus, the genus "less Developed Country" or "LDC" ' (p.55). Yet, argues Ferguson, there is an inevitability to this sort of misrepresentation for development agencies have to create semblances of situations which fit their solutions rather than vice versa. The problem with academic representations of Lesotho is that they fail to provide development agencies with the right kind of problems which can be tackled through the standard aid packages which agencies have at their disposal. Thus, to see Lesotho as a country of migrant laborers dependent on work in the South African mines, to see agriculture as little more than 'scratching around on the land', and to see Lesotho's problems as being in part the result of its integration into the regional southern African economy, is not useful to donors seeking technical and a political interventions. And this, argues Fergurson, is characteristic of how development agencies define the objects of their activities. LCD's must be 'aboriginal' in that what development involves in the modern world of roads, education, market and so on; they must be agricultural so that they can be developed through technical improvements; they have to be seen as national economies so that national plans can be evolved; and they must be governable in terms of an idea that the government is in control and works in a rational manner for development (71-72).

In his detailed discussion of the history of the Canadian-funded Thaba Tseka project, Ferguson shows how the design was determined by the same 'development problematic' he identified in his analysis of the World Bank document. The picture which emerges in the project documents is of Thaba Tseka as an 'an isolated, backward, agricultural economy which stands to be completely transformed by some combination of technical inputs, new knowledge and infrastructure' (p.86). Of course, this was far from the truth; even 'remote' Thaba Tseka was fully integrated into the market economy, and the 'backwardness' of the area was a direct results of this integration.

Not surprisingly, given the assumptions upon which the project was founded, it failed to achieve its goals. One of the most striking areas here was its failure to introduce new and improved forms of livestock management. Here, the project argued that what was needed to 'modernize' Thaba Tseka was to introduce new breeds of cattle and reduce the numbers of cattle being pastured on the degraded uplands of Lesotho. In other words, the road to development was a matter of the right technology. The attempts failed, mainly because the project failed to understand the role of cattle in Lesotho, in particular gender distinctions in livestock ownership and the importance of cattle to migrant men as a store of wealth and an insurance policy against old age. The stress on owning cattle and their symbolic importance was not some legacy of 'tradition' but rather an active response to the contemporary realities of migration labor. Only if Lesotho was viewed as a backward agricultural society could the project's policy be thought to be viable.

The second area in which the project failed to achieve its goals was in the field of administrative change. Here, the main was to generate what was called an 'Integrated Rural Development Project' in which various government ministries came under the control of the project with the idea that this reform of government activities would form the basis for more widespread decentralization throughout local government in Lesotho. Once again the project failed to achieve its goals, this time because of the political structure into which it was inserted. But, writes Fergurson, what is most striking about project activities in this area of activity is not that project staff were unaware of the political morass into which the project had sunk but rather that 'the project, by its nature, was not equipped to play the political game it suddenly found itself in the midst of' (p. 226).

The project's experience of decentralization only highlights what to Ferguson is central about the discourse of the development industry: that it attempts to reduce poverty and powerlessness to technical problems rather than recognize them as the result of political forces. Development discourse becomes a means of denying politics -- the anti politics machine -- but in the process of doing so actually increases the power of state bureaucracies. In a fascinating and thought-provoking section on 'etatization' he suggests that the activities of the development industry do not necessarily increase the power of the state but rather increase the powers of those bureaucracies which ostensibly work to promote development. The result is a 'knotting or coagulation of power' which is the 'development state' (p.274).

Ferguson writes as an academic anthropologist who does not see his role as a matter of trying to improve the effectiveness of the development industry. Indeed, given the logic of his analysis there is no way in which its effectiveness could be improved in terms of alleviating poverty or powerlessness unless the whole structure of the development industry's approach is radically transformed. Perhaps the least satisfying chapter of what is otherwise an extremely impressive book in a postscript in which he advocates personal solutions for anthropologists through becoming involved in non-state and counter-hegenomic organizations. Yet, even then, he admits that this will not have much impact of the development industry.

Porter and his co-authors of Development on Practice come from a rather different position. Although two of the authors are now academics, all were involved at one time or another in the subject of their book, the Magarini Settlement Project in Kenya.[7] Whilst writing as absorbing and intellectually satisfying book as Ferguson, they write from within the 'development industry' and, in part at least, hope to influence the ways in which projects are identified and implemented.

The Magarini Settlement project ran from 1977 until the final withdrawal of the donors, the Austrians government, in 1988. Ostensibly the project was concerned with dry land agriculture, an activity that the Australians were considered to have a certain expertise in, and the resettlement (or at least regularization of settlement) of people who had previously been engaged in bush fallow cultivation. As in the case of Lesotho project discussed by Ferguson, the Magarini project failed to fulfill the objectives laid down for it.

Many of the issues discussed by Ferguson are apparent in the Magarini case, and although the authors do not couch their arguments in precisely the same way, the manner in which the object for development is created through a particular form of discourse is again apparent. Thus, one more, project documents present the picture of a backward, remote population. The historical processes which gave rise to the particular distribution and agricultural activities of the population are ignored: 'it is almost as if they dropped out of the sky a few weeks' before the project appraisal' (p.45). The political structures of Kenya were only dealt with in a cursory manner and the project defined in a narrow technical fashion: if the technology was correct then the project would flourish. Indeed, such was the sway of the 'development discourse' that the official project list of the needs of

Local people 'systematically blocked' any discussion of what the local people saw as their needs (p.149).

The central theme of the book is that the Magarini project, like many others, was strongly influenced by what the authors call, 'control-orientation': 'the belief that current events and various states of land, labor technology and capital can be manipulated according to causal relations which exist between them, to achieve a desired objective in a controlled and predictable manner' (p.4-5). Whilst such an approach may be viable when building a dam or a power station, they argue that it is the 'antithesis of good development practice' when one is dealing with projects which involve people (p.92). In effect, they argue that there are too many unknowns, too many variables, for control-oriented projects to work, and they show in great detail how in the Magarini project a focus on control led to a fragmentation of the project, a stress on crisis management as the project lurched from one disaster to another, and its ultimate failure to achieve its goals. Indeed, the people the project was meant to benefit were worse off after the project ended than they had been at the beginning.

The examples they give of the failure of 'control orientation' are striking. Thus one of the problems which ran through the whole project was a shortage of labor for the sorts of agriculture envisage in advance by the project. These problems, which perhaps could have been identified, were dealt with in ways which only exacerbated other problems, for instance the use of mechanics means of ground clearance which had negative environmental impacts. Another was the use of cost-benefit analysis, logical frameworks and other techniques which, although giving a semblance for control, are in fact extremely poor predictors and bases for action. Throughout the history of the project activities were identified and implemented under the misapprehension that project staff were in control of the situation. Furthermore, the shift in the late 1970s and 1980s towards an interest in 'basic needs', growth with redistribution;, and so on, only made things worse in that they introduced new and even more complex variables.

Both Ferguson and the authors of Development in Practice make it clear that they are talking about the development industry at the particular time: the late 1970s and the early 1980s. Since the mid-1980s there have been changes. As far as the 'control orientation' discussed by Porter and his co-authors is concerned, there is a movement away from so-called 'blueprint projects' in which an attempt is made to identify all relevant variables in advance, and to plot out in detail the future progress of a project, to 'process projects' in which there is much less of an attempt to identify all elements of a project in advance.

Instead, stress is placed on the importance of flexibility in decision-making and the greater involvement of the supposed beneficiaries in the planning and implementation of projects. How successful this shift will be in practice in another matter. In practice there is still an emphasis on control which arises from the calls for accountability and the intrinsic logic of cost-benefit analysis.

The 'development discourse' has also changed over the last few years. Although the basic structure of the discourse Ferguson describes is still true, there have been some modifications which are seen by the agencies involved as a major shift in priorities. Over the last decade gender and poverty have been increasingly important, as have vaguely defined concepts such as participants and empowerment. Most recent, with the changes in world politics succeeding the collapse of the USSR, is the new -found stress on 'good government', a stated interest in human rights, and a stress on political conditionality.[8] Today a new feature of LDCs has been added to those listed by Ferguson: an LDC by its nature is subject to weak, corrupt, and undemocratic government. Yet what is striking about the new discourse of development is that now as in the past, the stress is upon technical solutions to underdevelopment. Thus the governmental problems are identified as being soluble by technical means such as aid and expertise to set up democratic elections, the privatization of segments of the public sectors and support for legal training. But this continues to ignore politics, history and culture, indeed, all those features of 'underdeveloped countries' which the preconceived models of development employed by the donors fail to recognize.[9]Ferguson remarks that, 'Many reports on Lesotho look as though they would work nearly as well with the word 'Nepal' systematically substituted for Lesotho' (p.70). Many development practitioners would agree, but not always self critically. After all, both are small, mountainous and underdeveloped countries.

At the same time, the sorts of politics machinations and processes described in both books will continue to hamper and limit the ability of donors to fulfill their plans. The recipients learn to use the discourse of development as fast as the donors, and there are few bureaucrats in the developing world who can reel off the current buzzwords as fast as the representatives of the donors. There is already a sizable literature on resistance to colonial powers. So far, the same sort of literature has been slow to evolve on local resistance to the aid industry. But when it does, it will have to include not just the poor people of Magarini, worse off grandiose ranching schemes; it will also have to deal with the bureaucrats, politicians and local administrators, themselves caught in a system not of their own making -- and this, not for the first time in history.

Source: R. L. Stirrat. Developing Africa? (*African Affairs*). Vol. 92 No. 367. April 1993, pp. 294-300. Used by permission.

Questions

1. What is your view about donors' on of development?
2. Should donors rely solely on information presented to by World Bank or should they conduct they own studies?
3. Do agree with Fergurson that most studies do not
represent the reality and are just meant for academic purposes rather than solving intended problems?
4. What role should a government play in a project development?
5. Was Lesotho's Government role in the project in line with your answer to previous question?
6. How would an anthropologist's arguments differ from that of an economist in the analyzing Thaba Tseka project?
7. Why do you think the two projects, Thaba Tseka and Magarini shared the same remedies yet they were operated by different experts and are located in different regions?
8. "An LDC by its nature is subject to weak, corrupt, and undemocratic government." Discuss this statement in reference to these and other projects you know.
9. What conclusion can you make from these two projects about outside management and neglecting local inhabitants?
10. Who should be blamed for poor management of the projectis, African or outsiders? explain.

Chapter Six

DROUGHT AND FAMINE: WHO IS RESPONSIBLE?

Drought and famine have become two inseparable brothers in Africa. Each country faced with a prolonged drought has suffered from some form of famine. To some, the drought has been too severe leading to many unpredictable situations. Thousands of people, animals and crops have either died or disappeared from the face of the earth as a result of drought and famine. Thousands of refugees are spread all over Africa due to lack of food in their homes. Forests have disappeared as a result of fire destroying thousands of acres formerly covered with soils. This has exposed once thick forests to strong winds and erosion. Rich top soil has been washed away in many parts of Africa leaving only bare stones which can rarely support any population. According to Lester R. Brown, the author of the *Twenty-Ninth Day: Accommodating Human Needs and Numbers to the Earth's Resources,* Africa is losing the battle to feed itself. Malnutrition and hunger are on the increase. He notes that the fact that many Africans are starving today is a stragedy. But an even greater stragedy is the fact that African governments and the international community are doing so little about the causal factors. In many countries, food-price policies are designed to pacify urban consumers rather that to stimulate development in the countryside. Except of a few countries such as Kenya, soil conservation programs are largely nonexistent (in *State of the World*, 1985: 38-39).

Throughout the African continent, people are struggling to survive. For decades, the mother land has refused to produce enough food for her children. A wide spread natural disaster in form of drought has scourged the continent. Countries like Sudan, Ethiopia, Chad, Zimbabwe, Zambia, Mozambique and Angola have   famine and drought tales to tell. They had tasted the fate of drought and famine with much hopelessness as each day has brought more death and pain among the communities. Traditional rituals and other practices have not stopped the drought or given much hope to the suffering. Some times, short rains have brought false hopes. Farmers thinking that finally the heavy rains   have come prepare their fields and plant maize, millet, sorghum, beans, and many other subsistence crops. But they are disappointed as rains soon disappear and are followed by scourging heat from hot sun which kills all the plants. The farmers are devastated and left with nothing to plant having planted the last of their seeds. As they watch desperately to their dying crops, they cannot resist shedding tears as the farmers foresee even more disaster and death. Without knowing when the next rain season will come, the cry to the world for food is inevitable.

Why Drought and Famine?

Many reasons have been associated with drought and famine in Africa like elsewhere in the world. To the environmentalists, this is due to de-forestation resulting from forests and clearing of once fertile land. The soil is exposed to   dense winds and rain leading to soil erosion. Similarly, poor methods of cultivation have been associated with droughts. The methods used, for instance, shift cultivation, top-down hill cultivation and   poor tree planting methods are major reasons for drought in many parts of the continent. To the climatologists, global warming has affected the winds and air mass movements causing the central part of the globe to be warmer and drier. Chemical poisoning of the environment has also affected the ozone layer in the atmosphere. Much destruction is feared that might lead to further warming of the seas. Such warming would cause rise in the water levels in the seas. In the areas already affected by drought in Africa, the situation is expected to cause more harm.

How Severe is the Drought and Famine in Africa?

Before 1960, Africa was self-sufficient in food production. In fact, most countries earned their foreign exchange currency from agricultural products. Until the late 1960 and early 1970s, most countries did not have any need for food aid. However, the last two decades have seen many parts of the African continent greatly hit by drought. In both the 1970s and 1980s, the continent's food production underwent some unpredictable changes. The production decreased delasticaly forcing most countries to import food to meet demand of their fast growing population. During the 1970s, food imported to Africa increased from 4 million tons to 24 million tons and by 1985, the continent was importing two-fifths of its food supply with almost a third of its people depending solely or partly on imported food. The period between 1980 and 1985 was one of the worst droughts in the second had of the century. In 1984 and 1985, in particular, about 6 million tons of food and $4.5 billion of emergency supplies poured into Africa in response to cry for hunger. Countries like Ethiopia and Sudan suffered severely. Even countries which seemed self-sufficient for a long time like Kenya had to buy more food to meet the challenge. By the end of 1985, more that 200 million Africans were at risk of starvation and death. Thank God the drought came to a temporarily end in 1986 and many countries promised to harvest substantial among of food, giving hope to many. However, the rains did not result much harvest as predicted. By 1987, food aid had to cost the continent amount worth $500 million (Jennifer Whitaker 1988:137). Even though the drought had declined, it had affected over 30 countries. The most hit were Ethiopia and Sudan where the cry for help caught the compassion of the developed countries with much pity. The media played a key role of creating awareness among the developed nations about the severity of the drought. This led to a positive reaction and food donations to thousands of sufferers. In fact, the issue of hunger had been forgotten in many developed countries before this time. Unfortunately, just as the issue hit the world outside Africa by surprise, it was soon forgotten as the cry was over. But the tragedy of those affected still remains. More that half a billion people continue to endure severe malnutrition daily in Africa. Many are too weak or too debilitated even to produce the food they greatly need. One wonder how long they can survive in this kind of environment. It is like digging their grave each day as they get nearer and nearer to their final breath.

To many in the West, the presence of drought to an extent of death for the local inhabitants remains a mystery. The Western nations having developed and progressed over the years find it strange to understand the situation. However, there is need to understand why the drought exists. Over two-third of Africans have land ownership of less than 1.5 hectares. With much of the continent being dry, farmers struggle to produce food and cash crops without any other means of production but seasonal rains. With the population increasing at the rate of 3 percent per annum, food production per person fell by 12 percent. It is not a surprise to find that poverty and malnutrition have affected the same farmer who struggle too hard to make their soil produce.

Most African farmers have no other source of income apart from farming. When farming fails, then it means there is nothing to sell, no source of income, no money to educate children, no money to buy food and no money to build any shelter. As a result, poverty becomes a reality of life to live and experience. Unfortunately, the mostly hit are women and children who live in the country side. Many nights passes without food as they look at the sky in hope to see a cloud of rain, a sign of life. In cities, most industries rely on agricultural products as source of raw material. With nothing coming from farmers, then lay-off of employees becomes inevitable. This increases the number of people looking for jobs in hope to get money to feed their families. It is a pathetic situation for those in a dilemma of life and death.

How Spread is Drought in Africa?

The spread of drought in Africa is so diverse that nearly every country south of the Sahara has had it share of the calamity. From Eastern African coast to Western Coast, from the Horn of Africa to the Cape of Good Hope, drought has been felt.

Looking at individual countries, the results show a great danger for the countries' future if the trend continues. During the last decade, for example, the mighty River Niger in West Africa dried as a result of the Harmattan Winds blowing down from the Sahara. This led to over three million people, dependent on the river to face great hardship. Majority of those affected were Niger's population. With little to do in the country side, about half a million nomads had moved to the cities by mid 1985. The number meant more demand for food, shelter, and jobs in the cities. Some cities like Niamey, Katsina, Hausa and Goure, were flooded with unrealistic population increase. Likewise, in Ethiopia, a country on the North Eastern part of Africa, about eight million people were affected by 1983-85 drought. Other countries like Kenya, Somalia, Sudan, Tanzania, Chad, and Zimbabwe also experienced a substantial degree of drought. In Sudan, the lowest level of the flooding of the Nile, the longest river in the World, was recorded after 350 years. In summary millions suffered in 1983-85 drought. In his research, Paul Harrison noted that by 1985 when the crisis was at its peak, about thirty million faced severe drought. Over ten million of them had to abandon their original homes to look for food (1987:18).

It is sometime hard to understand the severity of drought in Africa. However, close observation shows malnutrition among children and absolute poverty especially are the most acute physical expression of drought and its seriousness. To many Africans, poverty and malnutrition are overwhelming rural phenomena. Expressing this point further, Paul Harrison observes that in Tanzanian cities, only one person in five lives in absolute poverty while in the country side, two or three persons do. In Zambia, 24 percent of those in town are absolutely poor. This figure is compared with 52 percent of the rural population, people living under unbearable conditions (p.22)

The danger of drought in Africa is evident as Andrew Meldrum observes in his article entitled, "The Big Scorcher:"

> The worst drought of the 20th Century is burning up Southern Africa, exacerbating the plight of fragile economics. Hardest hit has been the region's table food, maize, which has been devastated from coast-to-coast, requiring the impact of 11 million tons of the crops. Some are now questioning the wisdom of being so dependent on a non-drought resistant food (*African Report:* May- June 1992:25).

As Meldrum notes, maize as a crop in Africa is proofing less resistible to drought. The failure of this crop has and will continue to have far reaching consequences. Millions of Africans across the continent rely on this crop as the only reliable source of food. The affected countries like Zambia, Angola, and Namibia have to import an estimated 11 millions tons of maize. This figure is expected to increase by the end of the century if the conditions do not improve. Statistics show that during the recent drought, Namibia alone has lost more than 80 percent of its maize production. This forced the government to spend substantial amount of money through importation of food. Similarly, Lesotho's maize production fell from 120,000 tons per year to only 45,000 tons while Malawi produced only 70,000 tons out of its annual 1.4 million tons per year (p.26). In some war which has left many people dead.

countries like Somalia, the effect of drought has led to international world cry. The situation has been worsened by civil. In his opening speech in the House of Lords debate of World Hunger on 13 July, 1983, Lord Seebohm, the President of the Royal African Society and the Editor of African Affairs, reflected greatly in his over 20 years experience and observations as senior executive of oversee bank operating mainly in third world countries. He said that world hunger is an important subject because we are not sure there will be any nuclear war, "but we do know that there will be more starvation. I guess that by the time this debate is over several hundred people will have died from starvation. It could be thousands." Seebohm further quotes Erik Eckhoholm the author of Down to Earth as saying that there were 68 million Africans who were believed to be under-nourished. This figure was about 15 percent of the entire population of Africa, yet "this is a continent where the world's greatest reserves of unexplored food production exist and where agricultural development can only be described as dismal." The author further says that the per capita output has declined by 10 percent in the last 20 years. The solution to this problem is agrarian reform, small holder progress, employment creation and dissemination of the means to exploit the means to exploit the opportunities which exit (London, 1982). According to the United Nations anticipation, the starvation in Africa is expected to worsen. With 470 million people in 1983, this figure was expected to rise to 2.2 billion by the end of the century. Indications of such increase in food demand was already evident by 1984 (*African Affairs* 1984:7). Africa's post war peak in per capita grain production came in 1967 at 180 kilograms. By 1982, it had fallen by 20 percent. In 1983 it fell an additional 14 percent because of the continent-wide drought. Although in 1970, Africa was self-sufficient in food, by 1984, imports had reached 24 million tons.

Even before the 1983-85 drought, nearly a fifth of Africa's population was sustained by grain imported from outside Africa (Brown 1985:23).

As seen, Africa situation has been deteriorating over the past few decades. The population has doubled while food production has continued to decline. Africa south of the Sahara has been noted as the only region in the world where food production per capita has declined over the period between 1960 and 1980 and food imports increased by 9 percent per annum. By 1983, African countries imported 40 million tons of food annually. The figure was expected to reach 72 million tons by 1990 and 100 million tons by the end of century *(African Affairs* 1984:3-7). The prediction was worsened by 1983-85 drought which made many African nations incapable of supporting themselves.

The Africans people have a saying that "a hungry stomach knows no avenues." It is hard if not impossible to reason with a hungry man. Many governments have tried to reason with their people in an effort to explain the economic effects of the drought. But the people have not seen the problem from the point of view of the governments. While the people expect their governments to provide food for the dying once, some governments have not succeeded. This has led to revolts in form of strikes, anti-government campaigns and political unrest in most countries.

Governments' efforts to curb revolts have only led to more oppositions in these countries. Both Zambia and Zimbabwe have had difficulties in controlling oppositions against food price increase, a thing viewed as a way of killing those already devastated by drought and economic upheavals.

African Beautiful Land

Rituals, folks, tales, and songs have expressed about the beauty of the Africa continent over the years. Beautiful environment: mountains, forests, rivers, valleys, lakes, and fresh air. Many legends explain how God gave the beautiful land to the African ancestors. Over the generations, the land has been passed from one generation to the next. This was done with utmost care to avoid annoying the giver, God. When there were calamities or epidemics, they were interpreted as people's punishment from God due to misusing God given land, or for abusing God's creations. In some societies, shifting cultivation was done to avoid injuring the motherland thereby making her bitter and causing her to refuse to produce desirable food. Even today, some communities consider land to be sacred. Many rituals are performed to appease the spirits who are treated as God's representative on earth. Through appeasing the spirits, land's fertility is restored. In many places, the current drought is associated with man's carelessness and misuse of the motherland.

Over the last decades, since 1950, the African communities have been forced to change their traditional practices and rituals. Many have adopted the Western style of living, a situation which has transformed the communities from their past practices to rely on new economical, political, and social structures. One of the major changes has been the reliance on traditional food like cassava, millet, and sorghum to new brands of crops. Also, the desire to produce crops for both consumption and commercial purpose has changed the life style of most Africans. And with many communities still holding the beliefs that children are source of wealth, the population has not been easy to control. As a result, it has not been possible to keep at the same level or even to match the population. With poor methods of cultivation and great desire to have more money to overcome poverty, the once sacred and highly valued land has been greatly exploited. The destruction seen in Africa today explains the root cause of drought in the continent although other factors like population and climatic change have played major roles. By 1987, some 3.7 million hectares of Africa indigenous forest and woodlands had disappeared.

The demand for more cultivation land has led to a gradual removal of dense forests. In West Africa, it is estimated that about 4 percent of the closed forest is cleared annually. In its report, the United Nations Environment programs estimated that a total of 742 million hectares which constitute more than a quarter of the continent is in the process of turning into a useless land for cultivation, or undergoing moderate to severe desertification. The report further observes that the deforestation and soil erosion are undermining the very resources on which Africa farmers depend on. The situation is expected to continue as demand for food become inevitable and out of control (Harrison 1987:27).

Due to the worsening situation in the continent of Africa, it is estimated that Africa's environmental crisis will deepens and perpetuate its food, poverty and financial needs. Such predictions not only just threatens hope of progress but expectation of survival for the inhabitants is endangered. This prediction is already felt and experienced from major corners of the continent as the need to liberate Africa from hunger becomes even more and more real.

Will Africa Survive?

As I reflects the need for food in Africa, as I focus on hunger, poverty and malnutrition in Africa especially among children and women, I ask myself, will Africa survive? But then I am comforted to know that with careful planning, organizing, and coordination of resources, the states of Africa can rectify the situation and create hope for the desperate. With commitment to afforestation, environmental control enforcement, for example, restricting burning during dry seasons, the continent can resume its original status. It is possible for Africans to feel desperate and forget their roles. However, such actions will only leave them at the mercy of the Western nations making the continent more dependence. Unfortunately, before the Western nations react to the mess done, often the African people have suffered greatly. This calls for another approach to the continent's environmental problems by Africans themselves. While the developed nations can and have helped many countries under poverty, they will rarely succeed in helping the continent which they rarely understand its deep rooted and complex values. It is time for the African to devote and sacrifice themselves to save the continent from becoming a desert. Survival in the future will depends on the strategies laid today, just like the past strategies have led to the much crisis in the continent.

Much of the leadership greed and self ambitiousness and lack of interest in development have to change into social commitment. It does not require leaders only to build Africa to a desirable continent, but all inhabitants.

To all the Western nations, Africa need foreign aid to solve both her short term and long term development crisis. The African states lack technologies, ability and means to shape the continent to its original state. It is unfortunate most aid and other assistance are not meant to satisfy the states of Africa but are tired to benefit the donors indirectly. The new approach toward development focuses on preventing immediate and wide spread famine already experienced. With unity among nations, with strict continental measures, the continent should be able to heal it self from destruction. The African states cannot change their geographical location on the surface of the earth, but they can change the surface of the continent to reflect the original beauty and productivity.

Showing the importance of African themselves developing their own workable policies, Mr. Pisan, the EEC commissioner responsible for the policy on aid and development visited several African countries which include Mali, Kenya, and Zambia. His message was that only a change of policies will enable Africa reach self-sufficiency. He said, only then was EEC be willing to provide Africa with inputs designed to implement the strategies. The strategies recommended fall in four areas: production and marketing, storage, transportation and structural measures. In right of these areas, Africa needs policies and strategies on food, fuel, afforestation, water supply, diversification and efficient management of domestic livestock. But Seebohm suggestion is that a global approach to the problem is vital rather than selecting certain areas or sectors. The need is to focus on areas which promise chances of success (pp. 7-8).

Although the Africans have to play a key role in rescuing the continent, the world especially the developed countries need to learn that while famine can be avoided, this is only possible with capital capabilities of African countries. Increased food production must be coped with an economic purchasing power of the rural farmers. Because African farmers have to grow and feed the rest of the population, they need to have the capability to purchase and finance modern methods of production. To date, most African farmers still use traditional methods of farming which yield less and less returns per hectare each year. While the international donors and other agencies have spent billion feeding the hunger stricken communities, they should spent much time and effort promoting development in rural areas. The African soil is already exhausted by poor practices of cultivation but with technical and educational programs, there is a hope of increase productivity. It is an increasingly world concern that third world development policies need to be targeted to the poor in the rural areas. By increasing rural people's purchasing and production power, then industries can grow in these areas. One of the major problem facing farmers is lack of storage facilities. When there is too much food supply, there is lack of adequate storage facilities. As a result, farmers try to get ride of the produce before they go bad. And with high supply in the market, prices of the produce drop only to rise when supply is less. By this time, farmers have nothing left to sell yet they don't benefit much from falling prices. Lack of storage facilities means that prices of the produces cannot be controlled. Often governments try to increase incentives by increasing prices of the produce. However, the law of demand and supply often have much effort and over shadow any government's effect to control prices.

The above argument cannot be complete without emphasizing the need for the African governments to be committed to rural development. There is a need to focus on the center of the economy which depends on rural farmers. Instead of crying for aid for their people and then keeping quiet once the hunger is over, governments have to devote their attention to rural development. Let donors see actions were people are.

The importance of alternative industries cannot be overruled given the unpredictable whether conditions of Africa. Service industries, for example, are becoming more vital in the world market. Computer services are becoming evident and necessary world wide. If Africa does not give attention to such industries, then it will lag behind. Other services include banking, distribution service and transportation -- land, water, and air.

In conclusion, let me say that when all is said and done, the ball is left to the Africans to decide on the best policy or policies. Much attention has to be given on the methods of production and storage. Attention has to be based on the future of the continent and its increasing population. The past decades have seen some resistance and low response to hunger crisis. By the time other parts of the world come to discover the problems, often many Africans are dead. Many governments may never give the correct figures of those who die. Sometimes, the figures never reach the governments as many die and are buried or abandoned because many traditional beliefs still resist attempts to reveal sources of death. But it is not the world that feels pain, it is the Africans. An effective solution will work for themselves and will benefit Africans as the primary targets. One thing that needs to be mentioned is that the farmers will not be motivated to produce if governments buy the produce at a price below the cost of production which is common in Africa. In 1986, for instance, in Cameroon, farmers received only 29 percent of the world market price of the coffee.

In many other parts of the continent, the practice is not uncommon. This discourages farmers who look for other methods of selling their produce at high prices. In Tanzania, the state marketing system was unfavorable to farmers who turned to private traders to sell the crops. When the Government attacked and cracked down the practice, more than 3,000,000 tons of various crops were left stranded in the field. A good system of production and marketing which is satisfactory to the farmers and the governments in Africa has to be established if production is to increase which in turn will lead to feeding the growing population. Therefore, for hunger to become a past history in Africa, there is need for unity and understanding between the governments and their people, a process which can result determination of the right strategies and milestones to solve African crisis. It is not who is to blame for the drought and famine in Africa, it is who is doing what and why.

Chapter Seven

POPULATION: IS AFRICA REALLY OVER POPULATED?

In the next 10 minutes, 1,800 people will be added to the world's population. In the next 10 years nearly 1 billion people will be added, bringing world population to over 6.5 billion. If population growth is allowed to continue unchecked, our planet will be inhabited by 21 billion people by the year 2050 (Seattle Times, January 16, 1994). The projections through 2030 are estimated at 90 million a year. China, which has slowing population increase, is projected to add 490 million people, reaching 1.6 billion by the year 2030 (February 16, 1994).

In the period, 1950 to 1990, the world added 2.8 billion people to the face of the earth. This is an average of 70 million people a year. Specific analysis indicates that the World population approached a 4 billion mark in 1975. It is expected to double to 8 billion by the year 2025. According to the United Nations projections, the annual increase of about 80 million people was to continue during the 1980s and was to reach its peak of 90 million by the year 2000 (UN 1981). Surprisingly, population growth rates tend to be great where basic needs are not met. This is true for most parts of Third World countries, especially in Africa were per capita food production has declined by 10 percent since 1970. As a result, the current global rate of population growth of about 1.7 percent (2.1 percent in less developed countries and 0.6 percent in developed countries) marks enormous original variations (Redcliff 1987:30).

According to *Global 2000* (1982) , as quoted by Michael Redcliff, in 1975, the total population for developed countries was 1131 million while that of less developed was 2959 million. By the year 2000, the developed countries' population is projected at 1323 million while that of less developing countries is expected to be 5028 million. This is a net growth of 17% for developed countries and 70% for developing countries (1987:30).

Almost half of Africa is affected by population growth. As early as 1975, the total land areas of Africa could not support its population. The critical areas include much of North Africa, almost the whole of the Sahel region, the most densely populated parts of East Africa, and a dry zone area stretching across Southern Africa. By the year 2000, less than 30 of the 51 countries in Africa will be unable to feed their populations. Their total populations will be 477 million, that is 58 percent of the regional total population, of which more than one hundred will be in excess of the land's carrying capacity (Redcliff 1987:31).

In his observation of the World population crisis, World Watch President Lester Brown noted that the world farmers can no longer be counted on to feed the projected additional number of people expected (*Seattle Times,* January 16, 1994). This greatly applies to Africa where farmers cannot be depended on to feed the increasing population.

For several hundred years prior to the twentieth Century, the total population of Africa seemed to have remained constant. However, during the present century, the increase in population has increased drastically and the continent now shares with Latin America the highest rate of population growth.

Africa, south of the Sahara, has high population growth than anywhere in the world. In fact, out of thirty-nine states, only ten have an annual rate increase of less than 2 percent, whereas fourteen have annual increase of above 2.5 percent. The most rapidly growing areas range from East Africa: Uganda and Kenya to: Togo, Dahomy, Nigeria and Niger in West Africa. It appears that these countries population will continue to increase into the future for at least one generation and probably for much longer. Countries like Chad, Niger, Mali, Burkina Faso, Mauritania, Senegal, Gambia and Cape Verde, have a population growth of 2.5 percent a year while food production has grown at the rate of only 1 percent. This means a gap of 1 to 5 percent has to be filled through importation of food. The natural environment is particularly vulnerable under these circumstances, as even small numbers of people can have a large impact of fragile entrainments and it is hard to increase productivity on poor soils (Redcliff 1987:66-67). One estimate, for instance, places the population in the year 2000 at 768 million, or about twice the 1975 size. In addition, though the proportion of the population urbanized remains small compared to the country side.

Africa Government and Population Growth

The African governments are increasingly taking account of projected population figures as awareness develops on the implications of current demographic trends on development. The need for improved estimates of contemporary levels of fertility, morality and the size of the national population at a base is emphasized by the number of occasions on which countries have discovered that their current annual population census estimates falls short of the enumerated total. All the African countries have laws and regulations which indirectly affect family sizes, population growth, distribution and movements. However, but the laws are less strictly observed. For example, by 1973, ten nations in Africa south of the Sahara had an official family planning policy -- Ghana, Dahomy, Nigeria, Sudan, Uganda, Kenya, Rhodesia, Botswana, South Africa and Tanzania. Of all these, only three countries -- Botswana, Ghana, and Kenya -- had official policies to reduce population growth. Other governments have not given much attention to the practice. The reason can be associated with traditional beliefs among many Africans whether in governments' or not. It is hard for government officials who have many wives and children to convince other members of the society to control their population. Leaders have to be a model for the society. Most African leaders are not in this particular area. While they preach one message, the practice the opposite.

Population and the Environment

As population grows, more and more natural bush is cleared for agriculture. Similarly, more and more herds of livestock weaken plants that cover the soil. This gives way to erosion. Once the vegetation cover is removed, Africa's fragile soils are exposed to strong winds and battering rains. This makes erosion inevitable. Losses of 20 to 50 tones of top soil per year are not uncommon in many cultivated areas. According to United Nations Environment Programme, an estimated total of 742 million hectares -- more than a quarter of the whole continent -- is in the process of becoming useless for cultivation because it is undergoing severe to moderate desertification (Harrison 1987:26).

African Traditional Beliefs and Population

In Africa, there had been a remarkable change in attitude toward family planning, much of its occurring in the early 1980s. The "frightening arithmetic" of population growth became a clich in the African capitals. It was in the national economic planning commission that the population threat surfaced most clearly. Falling per capita food production was now the rule, not the exception. The demographics prospect in Africa is equally bleak. As in most of the third world, not only is population growth rapid, but the number of young people reaching adulthood is far greater than ever before. The World Bank projects that the current populations of Ethiopia and Nigeria, which is now home of 92 million people (1985) will increase at a rate high than anywhere in the world. The Bank projects an incredible additional 537 million people -- more than the current population of the entire continent. The projected growth for North America, all of the Europe, and the Soviet Union is less than the addition as expected in either Bangladesh or Nigeria (i*World Bank, World Development Report* 1984 (in *State of the World,* 1985:201-205).

Population and Development

By 1984, total African population was about 470 million. With an average growth of 3 percent per annum, Burkina Faso has an average of 1.9 while Cote d'Ivoire had an average growth of 4.6 percent. At such a rate, the population was expected to double in 23 to 35 years.

Table 7.1

FERTILITY-RELATED INDICATOR FOR SUB-SAHARA AFRICA

	Percentage of Married Women of Childbearing Age Fertility Using Contraception	Rate	Desired Family
Benin	6	6.5	7.6
Botswana	29	6.7	
Burkina Faso	1	6.5	
Cameroon	3	6.8	6.4
Cote d'Ivoire	3	6.5	7.2
Ethiopia	2	6.2	
Gambia	5	6.5	
Ghana	10	6.4	6.1
Guinea	1	6.0	
Kenya	17	7.8	7.2
Lesotho	5	5.8	5.9
Liberia	1	6.9	
Malawi	1	7.6	
Nigeria	5	6.9	6.3
Rwanda	1	8.0	
Senegal	12	6.7	8.8
Sierra Leone	4	6.5	
Somalia	(.)	6.8	
Sudan	5	6.6	6.3
Tanzania	1	7.0	
Uganda	1	6.9	
Zaire	1	6.1	
Zambia	1	6.8	
Zimbabwe	40	6.2	

Source: Columns (1) and (2) from: *World Bank, World development Report 1987* (Washington DC.). : *World Bank,* 1987): Column (3) from: *World Bank, Population Growth and Policies in Sub-Sahara Africa* (Washington DC.). : World Bank, 1986)[Reported in *African Affairs*, April 1988:268) Used by permission

From the table above it is clear that Africa has the highest rates in the world. Fertility is defined as the number of children an average woman would bare in her life time if she adheres to current age specific birth rates. In the Sub-Sahara Africa, the fertility rates range from 6 to 8.1 children. These figures though surprising to the world may not surprise an African woman who desires to have more children than she probably can bare. The maximum could be as high as 7.2 or more. Women in Benin desire to have a family of 7.6 while in Sierra Leone, a family size of 8.8 is desired. The desire is especially great among women who bare girls and feel cursed by the society for not baring boys. As they strive hard to have boys, they may end up having many children. The desire is not based on personal health but on societal pride and satisfaction. A man without a son feels cursed as he has no one to pass his wealth or to carry on his lineage upon his death. Until recently, women have been accused for not bearing male children. The belief is still strong among many societies despite medical claims that a man is responsible. It is difficult to convince many communities of the importance of family planning as this is seen as a Western style which interferes with African traditional beliefs. There is a strong link between the living and the dead (or those departed to the world of the spirit). In many societies, the ancestors decide when a woman should conceive, the name of child, and sex. The ancestors oversee the development of the fetus to its birth and its growth to maturity. Any effort by the living to control conception is seen as interfering and taking the role of the spirits and the ancestors. And these being the closest beings to God, then interfering with their roles and activities is like insulting God who directs their activities. Care has to be taken and proper treatments of the links between man and God.

To decide the number of children to bare is like taking control of one's life, something which is directed and guarded by the spirits of the living dead and the ancestors.

In modern times increase in population has generally been compatible with economic growth. On the balance, however, the effects on human ecology on large human numbers appear to have been highly beneficial in the past. Some have come to believe that although Thomas Malthus was criticized as being unrealistic in England in 1798, his theory is proofing to be applicable to Africa, several centuries later. The fact that food production has not kept pace with population increase has led to hunger and death which Malthus felt would be the only way to check population increase. But Malthus theory of population assumes nature taking its course in life control and does not consider technological development, something which can alter his prediction resulting much food production as compared to population increase. Malthus theory has been altered in developed countries like U.S.. This has led to higher food production as compared to population growth.

African Governments and Population Growth

Governments in Africa have tried to replace the traditional beliefs by educating the societies of the need to control families. Unfortunately, few societies have seen the connection between the environment and population growth. Until the last two decades which have seen wide spread of drought and famine in many parts of Africa, many people had little time to relate the two. Traditionally, drought and famine or other natural disasters were seen as punishments from God for poor management of resources, or sinning against God and his agents -- the spirits. Rituals and other traditional practices were carried out to appease the spirits and to ask for forgiveness. Governments' efforts to control family planning have been accused by many Africans as a method of allowing the rich to continue to acquire wealth while the poor, who belief in having more children in hope that one might be fortunate and become rich: thus assist the others. Take for example a government minister who often has more that two wives and many children addressing a community on the topic "let us control the number of children we are having." The society cannot see any sense in such a message and will never take heed of what he advocates. Unless there are practical examples from those in authority, African governments will rarely succeed in their efforts to control population.

Other failures of the governments to control population growth are associated with the thinking that the population questions started when most of the countries were under colonial powers. The issue is considered to be colonialist in intent rather that indigenous. These perceptions are relevant to the slow start and poor initial performance of Kenyan population and family planning programmes. Like Kenya, Ghana's attempt which started in 1969 has not been successful. However, with the changing trend in environment and economic situations, many Africans are starting to see a need to have few children. Governments could utilize this situation to educated and enhance the need for population control in order to achieve better living standards and generate future hopes.

Western Technologies and Population Conflict

Subsequently, the Europeans brought Western technologies that in themselves would radically alter the African world for ever. First of all, they introduced crops that would be sold in Europe. Africans were expected to sell to this new market and give less attention to their traditional crops. The Europeans also began to treat the Africans' illness with Western medicines. As more and more children grew to adulthood, the traditional balance between people and nature came under severe threat.

In the 1970s, the exploding growth of African population began to puzzle experts. While in Asia and Latin America better health care, extension of education and rise in income were accompanied by falling population growth, in Africa the reverse was observed. An improvement in the family health status meant an increase in the number of children born. The love for children made many Africans to see this as an opportunity to expand their family trees. In Kenya, for instance, in 1960, just before independence, the average Kenyan woman had 6.2 children. In 1970, she had 7, and by 1980, the figure had rose to 8.3 children (David Lamb, *The Africans,* p.7 as quoted by Whitaker, 1988:88).

Although population growth is seen as the root cause of most of the problems experienced today in Africa, critics have argued differently. Many have wondered whether population explosion is really the problem in Africa. Most African governments have opposed population growth as the root cause of African problems. At the 1974 United Nations Conference on Population in Bucharest, Romania, the African delegation passionately denounced Western view of family planning as conspiracies aimed at restricting the number of black inhabitants of this planet and keeping their countries small, poor and marginal. "You want us to go back to our villages and take your pill," one African delegate resented bitterly. "Why don't you listen to us for a change?" More broadly, the delegation argued that the African countries were under populated, with extensive unused land and such great distance between people that trade could not flourish. An Ethiopian Professor expresses very succinctly the traditional attitude toward people and land that still prevailed: "One is born; one dies; and the land increases" (Whitaker, 1988:89).

Like the leaders, most Africans still do not see any reason that they should not have as many children as possible. Few people care or spend much time thinking about the connection between their own decisions and the economic health of their countries. Africans are not however any different from any other people in the world and should not be seen as such. What is different in Africa is the combination of pressures and supports for unplanned high rates of fertility. In Europe, before the Industrial Revolution, scarcity of land, a new calculus of costs and benefits coming with the growth of the urban money economy, and constantly high mortality rates kept population growth at about 1 percent. In Africa, on the other hand, the introduction of modern life style and technology brought better health but almost no visible change in desire for even larger families.

Unlike their counterparts in Asia and Latin America, many African women put no limit on the number of children they desire to bear (p.89), and are not greatly concerned with the issue of population control which is termed as political, not social.

Consequence of Population explosion

With a fast growing population pressure, there is increasing reason to question the traditional opinion that land is abundant in Sub-Sahara Africa. There are many regions where considerable amount of land exists for expanding the areas under cultivation. This demands expensive infrastructures in the form of roads, other modes of transportation, and communications. There is already indications of pressure on the traditional farming systems because of the growth in population and extended cultivation. Studies carried out in many African regions report that fallow periods have been reduced substantially to accommodate the great need for food, leading to a decline in soil fertility. With the rapid rate of population growth, it is not surprising that an increase in the number of rural areas under cultivation in Sub-Sahara Africa are beginning to feel population pressure. Land scarcity and lack of employment in many densely populated areas have led to a shift of population to semi-arid and other marginal areas where land is still available. Unfortunately, such areas do not promise much hope as they have little rains and production can be very unpredictable. Some examples of such densely and potential farming areas forcing inhabitants to look for land elsewhere include: Kisii highlands, Kiambu, Murang'a, Nyeri -- in Kenya; Kigezi in Western Uganda; Ibo land in Nigeria; and the coastal area of Western Africa especially Ghana.

A dramatic symptom of the growing population pressure in Africa is the emergence of large food deficits in some of the more populous countries. As seen earlier, food production has not only failed to keep pace with population growth, it has also lagged behind all other regions of developing world. Although this decline can be associated to unfavorable weather conditions facing the continent over the last two decades, it is clear that the traditional farming methods have been unable to respond adequately to the demands resulting from rapid population growth. Table 7.2 shows the indexes of food production per person in Africa as compared to other developing countries.

Table7.2

INDEXES OF FOOD PRODUCTION PER PERSON
1966-70 AND 1970-76 (1961-65=100)

	Average 1966-70	Average 1971 -76
Africa	99	96
North and Central America	105	110
South America	104	104
Asia	104	107

Source: From World Development Report 1978 by the World Bank. Copyright 1978 by the International Bank for Reconstraction and Development/The World Bank. Reprinted by permission of Oxford University Press, Inc.). (in *World Development Report,* 1978:52)

The future of food production in Africa is at a jeopardy. Unless other methods of food production are adopted, there is a danger of much death in Africa. Comparing that more than half of Africa's population is under 15 years of age, and considering that the available land is not able to meet even the current demand for food, then the survival for the future is uncertain for the children, both present and unborn.

In the current situation in Africa, the majority of people have accepted the need for changes in population. What is now required are resources to transform the positive attitude into reality. In his observation, Fred T. Sai, a senior advisor in Population and Human Resources Department at the World Bank, in his article, *Changing Perspectives of Population in Africa and International Responses,* the major need for implementation of policies is financial. He however, noted that family planning activities are not very much intensive activities compared with many other development efforts. The activities require much more human capital, more thinking and more reorientation, or education efforts. He sees major needs as being that of funds for contraceptives, equipment, and vehicles to carry family planning workers and supplies around. He observes that by 1981, the international official assistance in population field was about 500 million dollars. Much effort has been put in data bases about population in Africa. There is a need to make use of the data rather than spending too much time gathering data that in most cases is never used. Data that is meant to put in place the programmes and operations that would make family planning effective is what Africa needs (in *African Affairs*, 1987:275-276).

Let me point out that although it is greatly felt that development can be achieved by controlling population growth to an acceptable level, we need to understand that the poor people do not just decide to have children. Without much hope for survival, the poor adopt large family strategy as the only form of ensuring their existence. As long as these people remain poor, all efforts to control population will continue to be frustrated. Success will be achieved through meeting the basic human needs as the first step in development. Governments should employ methods that will create hope in the communities and divert their minds from children. Education and other development projects could be the first steps creating such hopes.

Focus on Cairo Population Control Conference, 1994

The need to control population has reached a state where it need to be enforced. All world countries now agree that measures to curb population are necessary. However, how to use different methods of population control have led to wide controversy. Most religious organizations have opposed scientific means of population control especially abortion. The Catholic church is especially singled as a major opponent of abortion.

Although there is controversy as to the best methods of controlling population, the world at large recognizes the danger of high population. Realizing that women are key to any success in population control, the Clinton administration intends to guarantee thar family-planning services are available to all women in the world by the year 2000. According to the State Department Counselor, Timothy Wirth, population-control efforts are viewed as essential to improving the economic well-being of the world's have-nots. It is also a mean of protecting the environment. Wirth expressed fear that if the population is not controlled, it will double in the next 35 to 40 years and move to 13 billion to 15 billion people. "To imagine a world in which the population doubles in this fashion is unfathomable . . . and clearly does not allow us anyway that we're going to be able to maintain the quality of life or respect for individuals that are fundamental to what we believe in the United States" (*Seattle Times,* January 12, 1994). The administrations strategy to reduce population centers by first ensuring that couples and individuals have the ability to exercise their right to determine freely and responsible the size of their families; second, the administration aims at promoting access to all full range of reproductive health and family-planning services (including safe abortion services) while emphasizing the importance of quality of care. There is also the plan to support the empowerment of women. The focus is particulary centered on education. The goal is anable all societies move toward full gender equality in all aspects of decision making concerning economic and social development, and finally, the administration aims at ensuring access to primary health care, with an emphasis on child survival.

The administration's commitment to the strategies is clearly demonstrated by increase in financial support to foreign population assistance. In fact, for the first time, the administration's population assistance through United Nations Population Fund is expected to exceed U.S. $ 500 million (*Seattle Times,* February 16, 1994).

The Cairo 1994 Population Control Conference supported the U.S. call to control population increase. The Conference which ended on September 13, 1994 agreed on adopting major strategies to curb world population growth over the next 10 to 20 years. The Conference agreed that the most effective method of population control is to provide health, education and welfare needs as expressed by the people themselves.

Focusing on women is central in population control. The Conference advocated the importance of advancement of women mainly be providing them with education and allowing them to have access to economic and political power. The final document of the meeting further noted that "all people have 'reproductive rights,' ranging from 'a satisfying and safe sex life' to the right to choose 'freely and responsibly' the number of children they will bear, and to 'have access to safe, effective, affordable and acceptable methods of family planning of their choice" (The *Washington Post,* September 14, 1994).

The major concern for the countries attending the Conference was how to finance and implement population control plan developed. The countries were mandated to bear two-thirds of the costs. Mostly hit were the Third World countries who already suffer from heavy debts. However, the U.S. government was quick to respond to the need expressed by these countries. The government pledged to increase its family planning programs in the Third World to $585 million by 1995. Other developed countries also increased their spending in the programs. Japan agreed to increase its spending abroad from $40 million to $400 million a year, while German pledged nearly $2 billion in the next seven years.

It is believed that the partnership developed by "the spirit of Cairo" will bring the population to a reasonable level. The nearly 180 countries attending the Conference left the meeting with much faith that they had solved the world "Population Bomb".

CASE STUDY 7.1

Two Million Villages

THIS CASE   APPEARED IN DR. E. F. SCHUMACHER'S BOOK. DR.
SCHUMACHER IS A WELL KNOWN AS THE ORIGINATOR OF THE CONCEPTS
OF INTERMEDIATE TECHNOLOGY FOR DEVELOPING COUNTRIES, AND AS
ECONOMIC ADVISER TO THE NATIONAL COAL BOARD FROM 1950 TO
1970. DR. SCHUMACHER HAS GIVEN MANY LECTURERS SOME OF WHICH
ARE REPORTED IN SMALL IS BEAUTIFUL. DUE TO HIS INNOVATIVE IDEAS
AND THEORIES, SCHUMACHER SOCIETY WAS FORMED TO CONTINUE AND
DEVELOP THE CONCEPTS FURTHER. THE PRINCIPLES PRESENTED IN THIS
CASE ARE APPLICABLE EVERYWHERE IN THE WORLD AND THE DEVELOPED
AND DEVELOPING COUNTRIES SHOULD FIND COMFORT IN APPLYING THEM.

The results of the second development decade will be no better than
those of the first unless there is a conscious and determined shift of
emphasis from goods to people. Indeed, without such a shift the
results of aid will become increasingly be destructive.

If we talk of promoting development, what have we in mind --
goods or people? If it is people -- which particular people? Who are
they? Where are they? Why do they need help? If they cannot get on
without help, what, precisely, is the help they need? How do we
communicate with them? Concern with people raises countless
questions like these. Goods, on the other hand, do not raise so many
questions. Particularly when econometricians and staticians deal with
them, goods even cease to be anything identifiable, and become GNP,
imports, exports, savings, investment, infrastructure, or what not.
Impressive models can be built out of these abstractions, and it is rarity
for them to leave any room for actual people. Of course, 'populations'
may figure in them, but as nothing more than a mere quantity to be
used as a divisor after the dividend, i.e., the quantity of available
goods, has been determined. The model then shows that 'development',
that is, the growth of the dividend, is held back and frustrated if the
divisor grows as well.

It is much easier to deal with goods than with people -- if only
because goods have no minds of their own and raise no problems of
communication. When the emphasis is on people, communications
problems became paramount. Who are the helpers and who are those
to be helped? The helpers, by and large, are rich, educated (in a
somewhat specialised sense), and town-based. Those who most need

help are poor, uneducated, and rural based. This means that three tremendous gulfs separately the former from the latter: the gulf between the rich and poor; the gulf between educated and uneducated; and the gulf between city men and country-folk, which includes that between industry and agriculture. The first problem of development aid is how to bridge these three gulfs. A great effort of imagination, study, and compassion is needed to do so. The methods of production, the patterns of consumption, the systems of ideas and of values that suit relatively affluent and educated city people area unlikely to suit poor, semi-illiterate peasants. Poor peasants cannot suddenly acquire the outlook and habits of sophisticated city people. If the people cannot adapt themselves to the methods, then the methods must be adapted to the people. This is the whole crux of the matter.

There are, moreover, many features of the rich man's economy which are so questionable in themselves and, in any case, so inappropriate for poor communities that successful adaptation of the people to these features would spell ruin. If the nature of change is such that nothing is left for the fathers to teach their sons, or the sons to accept from their fathers, family life collapses. The life, work, and happiness of all societies depends on certain 'psychological structures' which are infinitely precious and highly vulnerable. Social cohesion, cooperation, mutual respect, and above all self-respect, courage in the face of adversity, and the ability to bear hardship -- all this and much else disintegrates and disappears when these 'psychological structures' are gravely damaged. A man is destroyed by the inner conviction of uselessness. No amount of economic growth can compensate for such losses -- though this may be an idle reflection, since economic growth is normally inhibited by them.

None of these awesome problems figure noticeably in the cosy theories of most of our development economists. The failure of the first development decade is attributed simply to an insufficiency of aid appropriations or, worse still, to certain alleged defects inherent in the societies and populations of the developing countries. A study of the current literature could lead one to suppose that the decisive question was whether aid was dispensed multilaterally or bilatelly, or that an improvement in the terms of trade for primary commodities, a removal of trade barriers, guarantees for private investors, or the effective introduction of birth control, were the only thing that really mattered.

Now, I am far from suggesting that any of these items are irrelevant, but they do not seem to go to the heart of the matter, and there is in any case precious little constructive action flowing from the innumerable discussions which concentrate on them. The heart of the matter, as I see it, is the stark fact that world poverty is primarily a problem of two million villages, and thus a problem of two thousand million villagers. The solution cannot be found in the cities of the poor countries. Unless life in the hinterland can be made tolerable, the problem of world poverty is insoluble and will inevitably get worse.

All important insights are missed if we continue to think of development mainly in quantitative terms and in those vast abstractions -- like GNP, investment, savings, etc. -- which have their usefulness in the study of developed countries but have virtually no relevance to development problems as such. (Nor did they pay the slightest part in the actual development of the rich countries!). Aid can be considered successful only if it helps to mobilize the labor power of the masses in the receiving country and raises productivity without 'saving' labor. The common criterion of success, namely the growth of GNP, is utterly misleading and, in fact, must of necessity lead to phenomena which can only be described as neocolonialism.

I hesitate to use this term because it has a nasty sound and appears to imply deliberate intention on the part of the aid-givers. Is there such an intention? On the whole, I think, there is not. But this makes the problem greater instead of smaller. Unintentional neocolonialism if far more insidious and infinitely more difficult to combat than neocolonialism intentionally pursued. It results from the mere drift of things, supported by the best intentions. Methods of production, standards of consumption, criteria of success or failure, systems of values, and behavior patterns establish themselves in poor countries which, being (doubtfully) appropriate only to conditions of affluence already achieved, fix the poor countries ever more inescapably in a condition of utter dependence of the rich. The most obvious example, and symptom is increasing indebtedness. This is widely recognized, and well-meaning people draw the simple conclusion that grants are better than loans, and cheap loans better than dear ones. True enough. But increasing indebtedness is not the most serious matter. After all, if a debtor cannot pay he ceases to pay -- a risk the creditor must always have had in mind.

Far more serious is the dependence created when a poor country falls for the production and consumption patterns of the rich. A textile mill I recently visited in Africa provides a telling example. The manager showed me with considerable pride that his factory was at the highest technological level to be found anywhere in the world. Why was it so highly automated? "Because," he said, "African labor, unused to industrial work, would make mistakes, whereas automated machinery does not make mistakes. The quality standards demanded today," he explained, "are such that my product must be perfect to be able to find a market." He summed up his policy by saying: "Surely, my task is to eliminate the human factor." Nor is this all. Because of inappropriate quality standards, all his equipment had to be imported from the most advanced countries; the sophisticated equipment demanded that all higher management and maintenance personnel had to be imported. Even the raw material had to be imported because locally grown cotton was too short for quality yarn and the postulated standards demanded the use of a high percentage of manmade fibres. This is not an untypical case. Anyone who has taken the trouble to look systematically at actual 'development' projects -- instead of merely studying development plans and econometric models -- knows of countless such cases: soap factories producing luxury soap by such sensitive processes that only highly refined materials can be used, which must be imported at high prices while the local raw materials are exported at low prices; food-processing plants; packing stations; motorisation and so on -- all on the rich man's pattern. In many cases, local fruit goes to waste because the consumer allegedly demands quality standard which relates solely to eye-appealed and can be met only by fruit imported from Australia or California where the application of an immense science and a fantastic technology ensures that every apple is of the same size and without the sightest visible blemish. The examples could be multiplied without end. Poor countries slip -- and are pushed into the adoption of production methods and consumption standards which destroy the possibilities of self-reliance and self help. The results are unintentional neocolonialism and hopelessness for the poor.

How, then, is it possible to help these two million villages? First, the quantitative aspect. If we take the total of western aid, after eliminating certain items which have nothing to do with development, and divide it by the number of people living in the developing countries, we arrive at a per-head figure of rather less that 2 pound* a year. Considered as an income supplement, this is, of course, negligible and derisory. Many people therefore plead that the rich countries ought to make a much bigger financial effort -- and it would be perverse to refuse to support this plea. But what is it that one could reasonably expect to achieve? A per-head figure of 3 pounds a year, or 4 pounds a year? As a subsidy, a sort of 'public assistance' payment, even 4 pound a year is hardly less derisory than the present figure.

To illustrate the problem further, we may consider the case of a small group of developing countries which receive supplementary income on a truly magnificent scale -- the oil producing countries of the Middle East, Libya, and Venezuela. Their tax and royalty income from the oil companies in 1968 reached 2349 million pounds, or roughly 50 pounds per head of their populations. Is this input of funds producing healthy and stable societies, contented populations, the progressive elimination of rural poverty, a flourishing agriculture, and   wide spread industrialization? In spite of some very limited successes, the answer is certainly no. Money alone does not do the trick. The quantitative aspect is quite secondary to qualitative aspect. If the policy is wrong, money will not make it right; and if the policy is right, money may not, in fact, present an unduly difficult problem.

Let us turn then to the qualitative aspect. If we have learnt anything from the last ten or twenty years of development effort, it is that the problem presents an enormous intellectual challenge. The aid-givers- rich, educated, town-based-know how to do things in their own way, but do they know how to assist self-help among two million villages, among two thousand million villagers -- poor, uneducated, country- based? They know how to do a few big things in big towns; but do they know how to do thousands of small things in rural areas? They know how to do things with lots of capital; but do they know how to do them with lots of labor -- initially untrained labor at that?

On the whole, they do not know; but there are many experienced people who do know, each of them in their won limited fields of experience. In other words, necessary knowledge, by and large, exists; but it does not exist in an organized, readily accessible form. It is scattered, unsystematic, unorganized, and no doubt also incomplete.

The best aid to give is intellectual aid, gift of useful knowledge. A gift of knowledge is infinitely preferable to a gift if material things. There are many reasons for this. Nothing becomes truly 'one's own' except on the basis of some genuine effort or sacrifice. A gift of material goods can be appropriated by the recipient without effort or sacrifice; it therefore rarely becomes   'his own' and is all too frequently and easily treated as mere windfall. A gift of intellectual goods, a gift of knowledge, is a very difficult matter. Without genuine effort of appropriation on the part of recipient there is no gift. To appropriate the gift and to make it one's own is the same thing, and 'neither moth nor rust doth corrupt'. The gift of material goods makes people dependent, but the gift of knowledge makes them free - provided it is the right kind of knowledge, of course.

The gift of knowledge also has far more lasting effects and is far more closely relevant to the concept, of 'development.' Give a man a fish, as the saying goes, and you are helping him a little bit for a very short while; teach him the art of fishing, and he can help himself all his life. On a higher level: supply him with fishing tackle; this will cost you a good deal of money, and the result remains doubtful; but even if fruitful, the man's continuing livelihood will still be dependent upon you replacements. But teach him to make his own fishing tackle and you have helped him become not only self-supporting, but also self-reliant and independent.

This, then should become the ever-increasing preoccupation of aid program's -- to make men self-reliant and independent by the generous supply of the appropriate intellectual gifts, gifts of relevant knowledge on the methods of self-help. This approach, incidentally, also has the advantage of being relatively cheap, that is to say, of making money go a very long way. For 100 pound you may be able to equip one man with certain means of production; but for the same money you may well be able to teach a hundred men to equip themselves. Perhaps a little 'pump-priming' by the way of material goods will in some cases be held helpful to speed the process; but this would be purely incidental and secondary, and if the goods are rightly chosen, those who need them can probably pay for them.

A fundamental reorientation of aid in the direction I advocate would require only a marginal reallocation of funds. If Britain is currently giving aid to the tune of about 250 million pound a year, the diversion of merely one per cent of this sum to the organization and mobilization of 'gifts of knowledge' would, I am certain, change all prospects and open a new and much more hopeful era in the history of 'development'. One per cent, after all, is about 2 1/2 million pound -- a sum of money which would go a very, very long way for this purpose if intelligently employed. And it might make the other ninety-nine per cent immensely more fruitful.

Once we see the task of aids as primarily one supplying relevant knowledge, experience, know-how, etc. -- that is to say, intellectual rather than material goods -- it is clear that the present organization of the overseas development effort is far from adequate. This is natural as long as the main task is seen as one of making the funds available for a variety of needs and projects proposed by the recipient country, the availability of the knowledge factor being more or less taken for granted. What I am saying is simply that this availability cannot be taken for granted, that it is precisely this knowledge factor which is conspicuously lacking, that this is the gap, the 'missing link', in the whole enterprise. I am not saying that no knowledge is currently being supplied: this would be ridiculous. No, there is a plentiful flow of know-how, but it is based on the implicit assumption that what is good for the rich must obviously be good for the poor. As I have argued above, this assumption is wrong, or at least, only very partially right and preponderantly wrong.

So we get back to our two million villages and have to see how we can make relevant knowledge available to them. To do so, we must first possess this knowledge ourselves. Before we can talk about giving aid, we must have something to give. We do not have thousands of poverty-stricken villages in our country; so what do we know about effective methods of self-help is such circumstances? The beginning of wisdom is the admission of one's own lack of knowledge. As long as we think we know, when in fact we do not, we shall continue to go to the poor and demonstrate to them all the marvelous things they could do if they were already rich. This has been the main failure of aid to date.

But we do know something about the organization and systematization of knowledge and experience; we do have understand what it is. If the job is, for instance, to assemble an effective guide to methods and materials for low cost building in tropical countries, and, with the aid of such a guide, to train local builders in developing countries in the appropriate technologies and methodologies, there is no doubt we can do this, or -- to say the least -- that we can immediately take the step which will enable us to do this in two or three years' time. Similarly, if we clearly understand that one of the basic needs in many developing countries is water, and that millions of villagers would benefit enormously from the availability of systematic knowledge on low-cost, self-help methods of water-storage, protection, transport, and so on --if this is clearly understood and brought into focus, there is no doubt that we have the ability and resources to assemble, organize and communicate the required information.

As I have said already, poor people have relatively simple needs, and it is primarily with regard to their basic requirements and activities that they want assistance. If they were not capable of self-help and self-reliance, they would not survive today. But their own methods are all too frequently too primitive, too inefficient and ineffective; these methods require up-grading by the input of new knowledge, new to them, but not altogether new to everybody. It is quite wrong to assume that poor people are generally unwilling to change; but the proposed change must stand in some organic relationship to what they are doing already, and they are rightly suspicious of, and resistant to, radical changes proposed by town-based and office-bound innovators who approach them in the spirit of: 'You just get out of my way and I shall show you how useless you are and how splendidly the job can be done with a lot of foreign money and outlandish equipment.'

Because the needs of poor people are relatively simple, the range of studies to be undertaken is fairly limited. It is a perfectly manageable task to tackle systematically, but is requires a different organizational set-up from what we have at present (a set-up primarily geared to the disbursement of *funds*). At present, the development effort is mainly carried on by the government officials, both in the donor and in the recipient country; in other words, by administrators. They are not, by training and experience, either entrepreneurs or innovators, nor do they possess specific technical knowledge of productive processes, commercial requirements, or communication problems. Assuredly, they have an essential role to play, and one could not -- and would not -- attempt to proceed without them. But they can do nothing by themselves alone. They must be closely associated with other social groups, with people in industry and commerce, who are trained in the 'discipline of viability' -- if they cannot pay their wages of Fridays, they are out! -- and with professional people, academics, research workers, journalists, educators, and so on, who have time, facilities, ability, an inclination to think, write, and communicate. Development works is far too difficult to be done successfully by any one of these three groups working in isolation. Both in the donor countries and in the recipient countries it is necessary to achieve what I call the A-B-C combination, where A stands of administrators; B stands for businessmen; and C stand for communicators -- that is intellectual workers, professionals of various descriptions. It is only when this A-B-C combination is effectively achieved that a real impact on the appallingly difficult problems of development can be made.

In the rich countries, there are thousands of able people in all these walks of life who would like to be involved and make a contribution of the fight against world poverty, a contribution that goes beyond forking out a bit of money; but there are not many outlets for them. And in the poor countries, the educated people, a highly privileged minority, all too often follow the fashions set by the rich societies -- another aspect of unintentional neocolonialism -- and attend to any problem except those directly concerned with the poverty of their fellow-countrymen. They need to be given strong guidance and inspiration to deal with the urgent problems of their own societies.

The mobilization of relevant knowledge to help the poor to help themselves, through the mobilization of the willing helpers who exist everywhere, both here and overseas, and the tying together of these helpers in 'A-B-C-Groups', is a task that requires some money, but not very much. As I said, a mere one per cent of the British aid programme would be enough -- more than enough -- to give such an approach all the financial strength it would possibly require for quite a long time to come. There is therefore no question of turning the aid program's upside down or inside out. It is thinking that has to be changed and also the method of operating. It is not enough merely to have a new policy; new methods of organization are required, because the policy is in the implementation.

To implement the approach here advocated, action groups need to be formed not only in the donor countries but also, and this is important, in the developing countries themselves. The action groups, on the A-B-C pattern, should ideally be outside the government machine, in other words, they should be non-governmental voluntary agencies. They may be sent up by voluntary agencies already engaged in development work.

There are many such agencies, both religious and secular, with large number of workers at the 'grass roots level', and they have not been slow in recognizing that 'intermediate technology' is precisely what they have been trying to practice in numerous instances, but that they are lacking any organized technical backing to this end. Conferences have been held in many countries to discuss their common problems, and it has become ever more apparent that even the most self-sacrificing efforts of the voluntary workers cannot bear proper fruit unless there is a systematic organization of knowledge and an equally systematic organization of communications -- in other words, unless there is something that might me called an 'intellectual infrastructure'.

Attempts are being made to create such an infrastructure, and they should receive the fullest support from governments and from the voluntary fund-raising organizations. At least four main functions have to be fulfilled:

The function of communications -- to enable each field worker or group of field workers to know what other work is going on in the geographical or 'functional' territory in which they are engaged, so as facilitate the direct exchange of information.

The function of information brokerage -- to assemble on a systematic basis and to disseminate relevant information on appropriate technologies   for developing countries, particularly on low-cost methods relating to building, water and power, crop-storage and processing, small-scale manufacturing, health services, transportation and so forth. Here the essence of the matter is not to hold all the information in one centre but to hold 'information on information' or 'know-how on know-how.'

The function of 'feedback', that is to say, the transmission of technical problems from the field workers in developing countries to those places in the advanced countries where suitable facilities for

The function of creating and coordinating 'sub-structures', that is to their solution exist.

say, action groups and verification centres in the developing countries themselves.

These are matters which can be fully clarified only by trial and error. In all this one does not have to begin from scratch -- a great deal exists already, but it now wants to be pulled together and systematically developed. The future success of development aid will depend on the organization and communication of the right kind of knowledge -- a task that is manageable, definite, and wholly within the available resources.

Why is it so difficult for the rich to help the poor? The all-pervading disease of the modern world is the total imbalance between city and countryside, an imbalance in terms of wealth, power, culture, attraction, and hope. The former has become over-extended and the latter has atrophied. The city has become the universal magnet, while rural life has lost its savour. Yet it remains an unalterable truth that just as a sound mind depends on a sound body, so the health of the cities depends on the health of the rural areas. The cities, with all their wealth, are merely secondary producers, while primary production, the precondition of all economic life, takes place in the countryside. The prevailing lack of balance, based on the age-old exploitation of countryman and raw material producer, today threatens all countries throughout the world, the rich even more than the poor. To restore a proper balance between city and rural life is perhaps the greatest task in form of modern man. It is not simply a matter of raising agricultural yields so as to avoid world hunger. There is no answer to the evils of mass unemployment and mass migration into cities, unless the whole level of rural life can be raised, and this requires the development of an agro-industrial culture, so that each district, each community, can offer a colorful variety of occupations to its members.

The crucial task of this decade, therefore, is to make the development effort appropriate and thereby more effective, so that it will reach down to the heartland of world poverty, to two million villages. If the disintegration of rural life continues, there is now way out -- no matter how much money is being spent. But if the rural people of the developing countries are helped to help themselves, I have no doubt that a genuine development will ensure, without the cruel frustrations on bloody revolution. The task is formidable indeed, but the resources that are waiting to be mobilized are also formidable.

Economic development is something much wider and deeper than economics, let alone econometrics. Its roots lie outside the economic sphere, in education, organization, discipline and beyond that, in political independence and a national consciousness of self-reliance. It cannot be 'produced' by skillful granting operations carried out by foreign technicians or an indigenous elite that has lost contact with the ordinary people. It can succeed only if it is carried forward as a broad, popular 'movement of reconstruction' with primary emphasis on the full initialization of the drive, enthusiasm, intelligence, and labor power or everyone. Success cannot be obtained by some form of magic produced by scientists, technicians, or economic planners. It can come only through a process of growth involving the education, organization, and discipline of the whole population. Anything less than this must end in failure.

*numerical figure was originally used for pound (emphasis mine)

Pages 173-192 from *Small is Beautiful: Economics as if People Mattered.* By E. F. Schumacher. Copyright 1973 by E. F. Schumacher. Reprinted by permission of Herper Collins Publishers, Inc.

Questions

1.What is the difference between people and goods?
2.What are the three gulfs separating people in a society?
3."A man is destroyed by the inner conviction of uselessness." Discuss this statement in reference to African societies.
4.Why do you think GNP could be misleading as a measure of development in developing countries?
5.How has adoption of imported methods of production and consumption led to neocolonialism?
6.Aid-givers need to appreciate the role played by those receiving aids and work together for a common solution. Discuss.
7.In a society where people are desperate for basic needs, like food, why should education be given much emphasis rather than the food they greatly need?
8.What has been the main failure of aid-givers?
9.Discuss how the A-B-C approach can facilitate development.
10.What is intellectual infrastructure and how does it apply to Africa?
11.Africa is largely hit by the problem of mass unemployment and mass migration into the cities, how can the countries tackle these problems?
12.Briefly summarize Dr. Schumacher's view of development as presented in the case.

Chapter Eight
THE REPUBLIC OF SOUTH AFRICA

Introduction

The Republic of South Africa has been a major focus of the world for several centuries. Occupying a total of 472,000 square miles, the country has a population of about 36 million people which comprises of: Blacks, 27.1 million (75%); Whites 4.9 million (14%); Colored 2.8 million 8%); and Asians and other communities, 1.2 million (3%). Over the centuries, these different groups have lived together and have played a key role in shaping the country's economy.

The presence of the Europeans in South Africa which made the country to be totally different from any other in Africa, cannot be understood without first understanding a brief history of their settlement.

Brief History Of European Settlement

The first group of Europeans arrived and settled in South Africa in 1652. Finding good climate and land, the Europeans (Boers), declared the country a Dutch colony. However, the British developed interest and seized control of South Africa from Dutch in 1806. During the 19th Century, the British controlled the country. During this period, the economic and political evolution took place especially after the discovery of substantial diamond deposits in 1867 and gold in 1886.

As a result of these minerals, the Europeans settlements increased dramatically. The discoveries also shifted the Europeans' dependence on farming which had been the main occupation, to mining and mining related industries. In 1910, the Union of South Africa made of both British and Boers was created. With Boers having much seats in the union, they had much power than British. In 1948, the ruling party declared the segregation and entrenched white supremacy. The segregation, known as apartheid, was still effective until May 1994 when the country, for the first time in its history held an all racial democratic elections. The elections gave the black majority more seats in parliament and enabled African National Congress (ANC) to form a government.

According to apartheid law, both whites and blacks were different and needed to be separate. The whites were superior while the blacks remained inferior and meant to serve the white people. In 1960, the Republic of South Africa (R.S.A.) was established. The country became a republic. This meant that the country became independent to have its own constitution and government without British or Dutch governments' interference.

Economic Strengths

Economically, the Republic of South Africa is the strongest and most diversified on the African continent. Investment, output, employment and consumption have been constantly rising. Until 1987, the standard of living was improving in all sectors of the society. Its Gross Domestic Product (GDP) per capita was about $ 1,900, which in the world economic ranking puts it with Yugoslavia (before the civil wars), Mexico, Malaysia, Portugal, Chile and Brazil. According to analysts, South Africa is said to expect a 4.5% GDP growth rate in the 1990s. Before 1945, mining was the backbone of the economy. After 1945, mining was overshadowed by manufacturing as the most important segment of the Gross National Product. Its industrial growth could be described by the fact that the country has cheap power. By world standard, however, South Africa is an energy intensive economy. It uses 28% more megajoules per unit of GDP than United States of America. The country is said to have probably one of the most sophisticated financial services, industries, banking and insurance, in the southern hemisphere. As a result, South Africa is the only economic giant south of the Sahara. This situation is expected to continue in the new South Africa.

The purpose of this chapter and the next is to examine the new South Africa and economic prosperity especially in relation to both domestic and international investments. To what extent have the international investments influence the country's development? What influence investments in South Africa? How far has United States' Government participated in the establishment of the current and past South Africa? What is the future of the country's economy?

Investments In South Africa: Local and International

Both local and international investors have taken a significant role in South Africa. However, as a consequence of the state's extensive intervention, competitive free market forces advocated by conventional Western Theory has never existed in the country. As a result, a handful of locally based mining finance houses, led by the Anglo-American Group, with ties to major financial and industrial interests in both Britain and the U.S. have played a key role in developing South Africa's industrial base. Most of the local industries have connections outside the country in one way or another. To ensure local investments were under its influence and control, the past Nationalist Government of South Africa broaden the role of parastatols in which it participated through holding its company, the Industrial Corporation of South Africa. Each of the Leading parastatal groups had its own complex of affiliates, many of them partially owned by transitional corporations as well as domestic mining finance houses. The largest South African parastatals developed with the assistance of Transitional Corporations are: ISCOR, the iron and steel Corporation, producing three quarters of the production of oils and petrochemical by-products from coal, IDC, the Industrial Development Corporation, and ARMSCOR which is government owned.

Foreign investments in South Africa take a bigger percentage of the economy. The investments started as early as 18th Century to date. In many respect, South Africa remains a peripherical region of international capitalism. By the end of 1970s, real foreign investments totaled to $ 20 billion. This made South Africa to be the largest single area of investment for the Western block. Britain led the field followed by U.S. and West Germany.

Let's examine the growth of some foreign industries in South Africa. The industries originate from major world multinationals.

The National Bank: The bank had originally been founded in 1890 as a central bank for the Boers' Transvaal Republic. Later in 1925, it merged to form Barclays D.C.O, one of the earliest transitional banks that operated through the British empire. Today, Barclays operates a large share of its business in South Africa.

The Anglo-America Group: This being the largest mining finance house in South Africa shows the symbolic relationship that has grown between transitional corporations, banks, the South Africa State, and domestic capital. By the 1980s, Anglo American had grown into an international giant, although its southern African assets still provided its financial foundation. Anglo affiliation penetrated throughout South Africa in mining, a limited amount of manufacturing, trade, finance, and real estate. It has also opened mines in Botswana, Swaziland, and Namibia. In virtually every case, it is still involved in exporting unrefined material to Europe, the United States, or Japan with assets totaling to more than $ 10 billion.

Anglo-De-Beers: This corporation controls 85% of the international production and sale of rough diamond. It mines diamonds in South Africa, Namibia, Lesotho, Botswana, and buy them from Zaire, Ghana, the Central African republic, and Sierra Leone. It ships many of its diamonds to Israel and Belgium where they are traded, cut and polished. Together, both Israel and Belgium annually export cut diamond worth more than $ 1 billion. Anglo- De-Beers has other major associates among them, Charter Consolidate, a British transactional which acts as its agent in London. Recently the corporation combined its U.S. interests into a new holding company, Minorca, based in Bermuda. It expanded its investments in the U.S. to become the second largest foreign investor in South Africa. Other corporations in South Africa include: British Petroleum (BP.), Texaco, British Rio Tinto Zinc and Dresdner Bank. All these and many other corporations have established themselves in South Africa and have no hope of leaving the country.

What influenced corporations to invest in this country rather than any other in Africa?

Upon coming to power following World War II, the Nationalist Party introduced new measures to encouraged foreign investments. Apartheid was also introduced. These two policies, although seemingly distinct, were intertwined. Attracting new investment was contingent upon guaranteeing profits which were realized by keeping black lower wages.

South Africa's major trading partners are U.S., Japan, Switzerland, Great Britain, and West German. British trade with South African declined from 29% in 1970 to 8% in 1984 while the U.S. shares rose in the same period from 8% to 15%. One reason behind the investments by these countries is the capital flows. This is enticed by a rate of interest which is as twice as high as the world average.

Another factor influencing investors to South Africa is low cost of production. The investors take advantage of cheap labor to do massive production and profit. The booming profits able them to strengthen their position in the world market. The investors are also able to curb competition and keep other investors outside South African market.

Why Invest In South Africa?

The are a number of factors explaining why United States and other transitional corporates continue to invest in South Africa. First is the corporates' desire to enter the large market. The South Africa's market is itself significant. Although the black community in South Africa has little money to spend on luxury goods, the 4 million whites constitutes an important market for high priced, manufactured consumer goods. This is possible because, besides being the minority, a fifth of the South Africa population, the whites' per capita income exceeds that of most industrialized countries of the world.

The black majority of South Africa have little capability to control the market or the economy. Overall, the cost of living more that doubled in the 1970s and almost doubled again by 1984. This reduced the real incomes of the black majority and narrowed the available domestic market.

Investment and Apartheid

The reasons for the foreign investments' expansion in South Africa, rather than in the independent neighboring countries, reach back into South African history. In the 19th Century, under the umbrella of British colonial rule, white settlers owned capital, accumulated to finance the development of the South Africa gold industry. Throughout Africa, mining investments remained virtually all foreign-

owned, at least until the new African governments obtained
independent in the 1960s.

In South Africa, the white settlers worked through locally based
mining finance houses to collaborate with international   financial
interests. As noted earlier, foreign firms generally get higher profits
in South Africa primarily because apartheid ensures that black
workers' wages remain exceptionally low compared to wages paid to
workers in other developed areas.

The parastatals sell basic units to corporates at or below cost. They
do this, in part, because they pay black employees low wages, in part
because they receive State subsidies made possible by the low level of
social services provided for black majority. By providing little social
security, health care, or education for the black majority, the state
holds down effective corporate tax rates to about 25% of net
corporates' income. From the favors given, the corporates benefited
greatly from Apartheid system and did little to oppose it.

But what is the atmosphere toward apartheid in South Africa?

The argument is often made that the loss of foreign investment would
hurt blacks the most. It would undoubtedly hurt blacks in the short-run,
because many of them would stand to loss their jobs. But it should be
understood in Europe and North America that foreign investment
supports the present economic system of political injustice ... If
Washington is really interested in contributing to the development of a
just society in South Africa, it would discourage investment in South
Africa. We blacks are perfectly willing to suffer the consequences. We
are quite accustomed to suffering (Seidman 1984:106).

As important as the psychological-political impact   liberation,
withdraw of U.S., investments would have another still more
important results. U.S. investment is South Africa is centered in the
vital sectors of economy, in areas where South Africa lacks natural
resources and a market large enough to make basic industrial viable
and the country self-sufficient. This is particularly true, for example,
in the oil and electronics industries. South Africa relies particularly
heavily on electronics and computers, to stretch the capacity of the
skilled white workers to run the economy and its large military
machine to obtain U.S. or other industrialized countries' electronics
technology, the ruling minority right (1994, *Washington Post Writers
Group*).

For a number of years, scholars debated the wisdom of boycotting South African goods and restructuring foreign investment -- some felt that such moves would bring the nation to its economic knees and force it to abandon apartheid. Further disinvestment was urged as a mean of accomplishing this aim. Most economists were concerned with the effect of such measures to the black population. It was feared the measures would affects black people economically long before it had the slightest effect on whites minority.

With divided opinions, it seemed the foreign investments in South Africa was long way from being terminated. Different opposing parties viewed the practice of apartheid as evil and needed to be changed.

United States' Investment In South Africa

In the first three decades after World War II, U.S. transitional corporations invested three times as much capital in South Africa as in the pre-war era. By 1983, total U.S. financial involvement in South Africa, including direct investment, bank loans, and stockholdings, had reached $ 14.6 billion -- equal to roughly two-thirds of the total gross domestic products of all neighboring countries combined. Direct investments totaled $ 2.6 billion, accounting for about 20% of all direct foreign investments in South Africa, and supposed only those of Britain. U.S. financial institutions had outstanding loans to South Africa borrowers totaling to $ 3.9 billion. Investors were estimated to hold $ 8.1 billion worth of shares in South Africa businesses, primarily mines. U.S. manufacturing firms had poured more that three-fourths of the capital they invested in the entire Africa and continue into building more factories.

U.S. direct investments in South Africa are significant not so much because of their amount, but because they are placed primarily in critical economic sectors that helped to transform South Africa into an industrialized and increasingly militarized state. Transnationals provide favorable international credit as well as technologically self-sufficient and better able to defy international sanctions. U.S. firms have played an increasingly significant role in key basic industries. This includes the motor vehicles market (30%), 44% of the petroleum products market, and 75% of the computer market, in 1980. Giant manufacturers like General Motors and Ford employed several thousand workers to manufacture cars, trucks, and components. Three oil majors companies -- Taxaco, Standard Oil, and Mobil -- refine and distribute oil products, helping South Africa evade the impact of the OPEC nation's embargo. IBM has 40% of the computer market while financial institutions like U.S. Chase Manhatta and Citi Corporation control finance in southern economy.

Why did the U.S. continue to invest in South Africa while it opposed Apartheid?

For decades, the U.S. government regarded Southern African region as of economic and geographical significance. Beside investing in South Africa, the region remains an important source of raw materials for U.S. industry, a role that will continue in the future.

The government has also focused on assisting local industries to grow. Through financial assistance, the U.S. governments has tried to lift the financial capability of the local investors. It may be a long way however before the small black businesses are at a position to compete with the South African Anglo American Groups or U.S. transitional corporate affiliates whose direct investments run into billion of dollars. Many blacks in South Africa viewed U.S. grant as designed to encourage the growth an elite black group that would accommodate marginal change rather that support elimination of the entire apartheid system. It was because of this kind of attitude that U.S. involvement was opposed. Will its role be opposed in the future too?

Chapter Nine

THE NEW SOUTH AFRICA: DOES IT PROMISE PROSPERITY FOR ALL?

The new South Africa is a miracle by itself. The way events changed so quickly left the world stunned and greatly amazed. Few ever thought black majority would have a country where they could walk, speak, and work freely. To many, a government of the blacks was a mystery and a dream far from reality. But the dream has come true. The blacks have a right to rule their country as do the white minority. A multiracial government is now in operation with its first black president, Nelson Mandela.

A grasp of what it felt to be free at last cannot be expressed better than was done by the people of South Africa as quoted by worldwide journalists:

"Why did we have to wait so long?" So many lives were lost, so many families were destroyed and the economy was in tatters before freedom arrived with the election of Nelson Mandela. "I've been waiting for this my whole life, . .."

". . .the election has had a calming attitude on South Africa. "It is so quiet," . . . ."all of sudden it just changed," . . . (*Seattle Times*, 1994).

However, not every one agreed that the task was easy. To some, the major task of rebuilding South Africa still lies a head.

"ANC[African National Congress] . . . is promising us jobs. Some of these things are impossible, but they are promising them."

"For us to turn the country around, it will take decades and decades," warned Tokyo Sexwale, a regional ANC leader.

"People think after the election, they'll get big houses and a Mercedes-Benz. And people believe that! I blame the politicians. They lie to the people." (*Los Angeles Times,* 1994).

The expectations from the black majority seemed beyond any government's capability in the short-run. The new government has first to ensure there is trust from all races in the country before it can engage itself in a particular constructive construction of the country. Most of the whites minority still in the country have expressed fear that the new government might turn against them.   As Paul Taylor of *Washington Post* (March 1994) interviews with some Afrikaners found:

> "As an Afrikaner, I feel like a sitting duck," said the soft spoken suburban housewife, anticipating life under the black-led government expected to come to power after South Africa's first election. . ."We're a little like Jews before the Holocaust. They also had their fears and hoped it would go away, but it didn't, and the whole world did nothing."

At a more domestic level, Afrikaners also worry about revenge resulting from crimes. "If I lived in a shack with no running water, and every white person had a home with two or three bathrooms, I would feel the same anger they (Blacks) feel now,". . .

"The next five years or so will be difficult because we are going to be paying for the sin of our fathers, . . . I'll be all right because I started out at a prosperous time. I feel sorry for young men and women just coming into the work force now."

"That was wrong," . . ."We spent a lot of money in this country developing our mineral resources, but nothing developing our human resources, and for that were are going to pay" (*Washington Post,* March 1994)

There is guilt, fear, and confusion as to what the future of South Africa may hold for the white minority. Having lived in the country for several centuries, their fear is evident. It will take the government more that mare words to convince the group that freedom is for all, not for the black only.

The New South Africa: Does It Promise Prosperity For All?   147

The transformation of any economy depends on the leadership. The world is watching closely as events unfold themselves in South Africa.

Investors are watching to ensure their interests are represented, just like the local population looks at the governments with much expectation of a bright future. In an article entitled, *Mandela, History Lessons Key To South Africa Success,* appearing in *Washington Post* editorial, "The beginning of South Africa's great good lack lies in the character of Nelson Mandela. His dignity, serenity and -- most important for a man now presiding over his former jailers -- forbearance stand in sharp contrast to the instinctive combativeness and mercurial moodiness of Russia's liberator, Boris Yeltsin." (May 9, 1994).

The government has to make sure the country does not become like many other African countries that have experienced chaos as a result of corruption and tribalism. Most African governments have been accused of corruption ranging from bribe, terrorism, and self-ambitions, meant to destroy their nations rather that develop. As Charles Krauthammer (*Washington Post,* May 9, 1994) observes:

> South Africa will face similar temptations. Disenfranchised blacks, impoverished by apartheid, will demand restitution. It will be tempting to try from the cities and give to the townships. In the short run, that would enrich a few. In the long run, any policy that provokes loss of confidence in the economy and / or white flight will kill the economy, whose robustness and expansion is the only hope for alleviating the country's crushing black poverty.

This brings us back to South Africa's first asset, Mandela. Because Mandela has been described as man of preternatural patience, he has a challenge to preach some of that preternatural patience to his own people. If he uses the economic crisis seen in the rest of Africa, he can explain, "that the injustices and inequalities of centuries cannot be erased in one year or one term or even one generation" (*Washington Post* May, 1994).

It requires great effort on the part of Mandela to convince his people that the New South Africa cannot bring fruits of prosperity over night. In fact, just like the people have struggled to gain independence, the struggle must continue in order to make South Africa independence a reality for all. South African must come together now, black, white and colored to reshape the country to a desired end. This way, the country will escape the chaos which faces many other coutries in the African continent.

Similarly, the new South African government has a great task of ensuring investors that the country is save and promising for further investments. The country has the best economy in the Sub Sahara region.

Realizing the great need for a strong economy and continue investment, Mr. Nelson Mandela, has noted that the first task of an a stable economy is ensuring that inflation is under control.

The government's five years plan calls for a variety of projects designed to improve black population living standards while promoting "overall financial stability" (*W-Journal*, May 1994). There is also a plan to give nearly a third of the country's farmland to the dispossessed blacks.

This particular issue was resisted by the former white government which saw this as ANC's clinging to socialist policies. But Mandela was quick to point that his party had moved away from nationalization and sought to reorganize the country's economy by satisfying the needs of the long-denied black majority rather than scaring foreign investors. ANC's other plan was to "build 1 million houses, provide all with clean water and sanitation, electrify 2.5 million new homes, and provide health care and phones to all the citizens" (*Associate Press*, 1994).

Mandela felt the immediate need was to implement certain key projects which included: free medical care for children under age six and pregnant women and food program in primary schools.

To ensure that the business community's interest in presented in the government, ANC has established a consensus approach and hopes to participate investors in key decisions (*W-Journal*, 1994).

The governments knows very well that foreign investments in South Africa have shaped the country's economy to a point that the country cannot do without them. While both black and whites have a role to ensure there is justice in this country, both need to examine the advantages and disadvantages of the both local and foreign investments and other government's institutes and see how they can benefit all without taking advantage of any particular group on the basis of its social, or racial economical divisions. The government's objective should aim at assisting the country achieve a stable political, social and economical level satisfactory to all races. That way, all can benefit.

A free South Africa for all races, means freedom from poverty, racism, greed, hate, anger and revenge. The blacks have suffered for centuries and the world knows this. Concentrating on the past can lead the country to a situation of chaos and regret. This can lead to blood shed and death, something all in South Africa should say is enough.

To develop the new South Africa, all races must work and live together. Development is a challenge and requires sacrifice for all. Let South Africa become a model of the rest of Africa. With its economic capability, the country can re-engineer economic reconstruction of its neighbors and later the rest of Africa.

Chapter Ten

A STRATEGIC APPROACH TO AFRICAN CRISIS

The economic problem in many developing countries is the development issue. The most outstanding characteristic of underdeveloped areas is widespread poverty and an associated low level of living standards. The main goal of development is to reduce poverty and raise the living standards of those affected. In many cases, greed for power, corruption, civil wars and unstable families are caused by poverty, an epidemic which has dominated a great majority in developing countries. It is not surprising that poverty has become a fact of life, a vicious cycle which is difficult to break.

While underdevelopment may be defined differently and standards of living may vary from one country or region to another, most African countries have virtually the same life style and culture. In many cases, however, development is seen as improving the living standard per se. This gives a general view of a country by taking the average income of both the poor and the rich. Income distribution becomes the issue of attention. As a result, the true meaning as seen by those affected is basically overlooked.

I will define development as a process of improving the total society. It is looking at a whole person rather than the economical side. To be developed means to improve and change the miserable, poverty stricken; it means feeding the people who know nothing about balanced diet because to achieve it is a myth. It means overcoming the problem of high levels of infant and child mortality; it means improving proper medical facilities and providing personnel to run health care programs; it means providing literacy   programs and overcoming the shortage of adequate education facilities; it means changing from living in shanties, hovels, and over congested environments,   to a healthy living. It is making life meaningful and hopeful. Unfortunately, a majority of the people in Third   World countries, Africa included, live in what can be termed as absolute poverty, and development is a foreign phenomenon that is only talked about by politicians and economists. I support Stockwell and Laidlaw when they say that:

> . . . the problem of underdevelopment is a human problem, not a statistical one, and that economic development entails much more than a simple increase in per capita income. It involves a substantial improvement in the social, economic, and personal well-being of the peoples now living in the underdeveloped areas of the world. . . in 1978 approximately 3.1 billion people (73 percent of the world's population) were living in underdeveloped areas (1981:28).

As noted, a great majority of people on the surface of the earth have only a vague imagination of what it means to be developed. While they may have food, a job, or water for a season, for most parts of the year, the people are faced with hunger, unemployment, thirst, helplessness and lack of hope. However, although this situation may be   seen as impossible to change, if well examined and managed, there is a solution and hope for the majority suffering in these countries.

Economists agree on four main factors as determinant of a country's development. It is only when these factors are fullfilled that people are considered developing or developed. The four resources are land, labor, capital, and technology. Most developing countries suffer from lack of one or more of the factors especially capital and technology. While land may appear to be plenty in areas like Africa, it is often bare and less productive. It cannot even support subsistence crops to feed the growing population. Take an example of a person who owns 500 acres of land in Northern Nigeria, a semi-arid region. The land is useless as long as it has not positive use.

The inadequacy of the capital in many African countries is evident to any person who has explored rural Africa especially during wet seasons. Lack of all weather roads make transportation difficult. It is difficult to access modern facilities such a medical, and schools. Farmers find it hard to sell their produce. As a result, there is plenty of produces that lot in the farms. This discourages the farmers who work too hard only to be frustrated.

The interrelation among different resources such as capital, social structure, technology, scale and transformation are complex. It is worth noting that the social circumstances surrounding economic activities of any sector affect in many ways the strategic elements advocated. Economic development established from within has a much larger impact among its implementors and advocates as compared to development imposed from the top or from outside. An open society which allows its members to participate in development leading to opportunity for social mobility results in positive attitudes which in turn result in high yields and increased productivity. This enables the society to have incentives for savings and for innovation - a key requirement for positive development.

If ideal was always right, then countries with large populations would be leading in the development process as the additional people could be used to increase productivity. This would enhance development as resources would be utilized to their maximum. Unfortunately, this is far from reality. Although most developing countries lead in population growth rates increase, they have a very small labor force as compared to the developed countries. While about 60 percent of the total population in developed countries is active labor that is used for production, over 60 percent of the people in developing countries are under 15 years of age. This leaves only a small percent of the population as active labor. It is this active population which is expected to feed and cater to the growing population of the young. In Africa for example, the labor force is greatly overtaken by the large population. Added to the problem of less labor in developing countries is the problem of lack of a technical skills. Most of the labor force is less educated and lacks the capability of most developed countries. As a result, skills necessary for the development of these countries is in extremely short supply. The following table shows the comparison between active labor in both developing and developed countries:

Table 10.1

SELECTED   SOCIOECONOMIC CHARACTERISTICS OF THE
POPULATION   OF   DEVELOPED   AND   DEVELOPING
COUNTRIES: CIRCA 1970

Socioeconomic Measures	Developed	Developing Countries	
		Total	Poorest
Percent of males who are economically active	58.8	49.5	49.7
Percent of working males with some kind of skill or technical training	47.7	19.5	6.3
Percent illiterate	0.9	63.7	83.2
Average per capita daily calories consumption	3,089	2,231	2,089
Percent of calories derived from animalprotein	41.3	9.8	6.1

(Source: Adapted from E. G. Stockwell, *Dimensions of Development: An Empirical Analysis, Population Review, 18* (1974):35-35. (quoted by Stockwell and Laidlay 1981:58). Used by permission of Nelson Hall

One major problem facing many developing countries is brain drain: whereby educated elite have migrated from their own countries to more advanced countries. This means that the countries have lost people they have invested so much in and this frustrates most governments. Most skilled personnel decide to work in the developed countries where they are paid well and also enjoy a good life as compared to their countries. It should be noted that most of these people fear to go back to their countries because they many not be assured of jobs. In some cases, they get jobs   which fall short of their expectations and skills and frequently offer low wages. Many developing countries have been hit hard by this problem because they do not have the capability to bring such educated people home. Countries have tried to put great restrictions on students before they leave their countries but unfortunately this often fails.

Added to the problem of inadequate active labor, less technical skills, and brain drain, most developing countries have faced a problem of poor diet thus poor health among the working population and others. As seen in the table above, the average daily calorie consumption among the more highly developed countries (3,089) is 38 percent higher than among the undeveloped areas taken as a whole (2,231), and as much as 47 percent higher than in the poorer of the underdeveloped countries (2,089) (1981:60).

In Africa, like other developing continents, the economic epidemic is a major concern. The consequence of this economic crisis is widespread poverty accompanied with extremely unbearable low living standards. Resources have either been over-exploited or poorly managed or underutilized.

Africans and others in developing countries have taken the blame and consequences of problems which probably they have had little or no role in creating. While most of the problems facing these countries are viewed as individual problems, let me point out that the problems facing these countries is part of the international economic crisis and the international community should not try to isolate the countries involved. If Europeans did not go to these countries at the time they did and if the Europeans did not exploit resources in these countries, we would have a different picture. Probably there would be no underdeveloped or developed countries. If blames and curses are transferable, then all those countries that took part in exploiting less developed countries would bear all the blame. They are the cause of poverty, low level of income and poor living standards, poor education systems and the like. As noted in the previous chapters, most of the present problems have their roots in the time when Europeans dominated these areas. Many of the problems can be traced to the growth of European capitalist economic systems where developing countries emerged as exploited suppliers of primary products that served as raw material for industrialized countries. The Third World countries acted as mining premises where minerals were excavated and once these were exhausted, the mines were discarded as useless. Unfortunately, after other non-human resources and humans were exploited, the Europeans abandoned the people to die and blamed them of being incapable of managing their resources. What was there to be managed? It is like setting a house a blaze and them blaming the owner for not living in a good house even though he may be trying to work hard to get his life together. In this case, however, after the owner has build another house, the person who set the first one ablaze still wants to control the new one. It is sad. Europeans set Africa ablaze and left but they still came back to control what remained.

The developed world has a key role to play in the development of Africa and other developing countries. Because most of these countries are still undergoing a restructuring of their economic and social systems, there is a great need for the developed countries to play a strong role in the restructuring. The developed countries must however realize that all the assistance they provide to Africa and other countries must be employed in such a way that the countries will have the freedom and autonomy to choose and manage their own path in the development process.

As for the developing countries, they should not focus their blame on the past but should exhibit their unique combination of economic, demographic, social, and cultural factors as they implement their development strategies. Each country can and should workout its own development program which fits its needs and circumstances. This does not mean that countries cannot combine and come up with a particular suitable strategy. To the contrary, unification of strategies and ideology can play a key role in regional development. This is especially possible given that most of the developing countries have similar or common cultural beliefs, climatic conditions and socioeconomic needs. Unification can play a key role in assisting each other where members can combine skills, technology, labor, and capital in a manner that can facilitate development. I will consider unification further, later in the chapter as part of coalition.

What then are the strategies to develop Africa?

African nations like other developing countries have fallen victims of exploitation both economically, socially and politically. Any positive change should lead to economic change, demographic change and socio-cultural change, the three key determinants of development.

ECONOMIC CHANGES

The goal of all countries should be to change their economy by increasing productivity and raising the level of living standards for their people. This could be achieved through the following approaches:

The first is agrarian reform. Most of the land in Africa has been exploited by man which has changed the environmental conditions of most parts. Consider the amount of land becoming desert each year as a result of burning, shifting cultivation, pastoralism and heavy rainfall leading to extreme soil erosion thus washing away thousands of rich top soil to the seas. As a result, most of the land is left barren and victim of heavy winds which carry the soil hundreds of miles away. Strategies such as land redistribution, improved credit systems to provide funds for farmers, and increasing the number of irrigation projects, can go far to improve land productivity. There is a need to restructure land usage and methods of cultivation. Strict laws concerning land burning to give room for cultivation need to be set. Governments should not be lenient on rules for land usage and should determine the proper methods of cultivation and farming. Shifting cultivation should be discouraged and if possible banned from Africa as this has exposed and cleared the deep tropical equatorial and Savannah forests giving room for desert expansion.

Secondly, the governments should focus on industrial development. This can be done through privatization and nationalization of foreign-controlled enterprises. In Africa, there is huge control of industries by foreigners. This leads to irregularity of businesses and improper monitoring of the industries. The governments can gain from these industries by having more local inhabitants involved in the business management. Another approach is to use taxes to assist local investors to start and promote their businesses. There is also a great need to encourage saving and investments among both local and foreign investors. Most foreign investors have used their position to exploit local resources simply because the governments are not able to control their operations effectively. They also use their position to threaten the governments to pull away from the countries if they are opposed in their operations. This makes the governments shrink as they fear for the people who may lose jobs should the foreign investors pull away. However, I strongly believe that the governments have been at times too lenient on these investors. They come to these countries because there is cheap labor and cheap raw materials and thus low production costs. With so much to gain, the investors cannot just leave unless they are totally sure they are losing over 50 percent of their revenue which can seldom happen. Governments should make their stand clear while at the same time, create a conducive environment for the investors but not through hurting the local investors. The governments need to remember that while the foreigners may leave any time, local investors will always remain. As such, all necessary means should be used to encourage and promote local investors. Methods like lowering taxes, offering loans and grants and opening opportunities for them can increase a country's productivity, thereby raising the economy.

Demographic Change

Demographic change has been observed to be a major threat to economic growth of the developing countries with Africa being in the lead. Because most of the beliefs associated with population increases are cultural and difficult to eradicate or transform overnight. A major strategy is required to develop educational programs that emphasize the desirability of having few children. Of course, this method has been used in some countries with little effect since. Those who advocate the methods maintain large families. Government leaders need to be devout and provide economic and social incentives to encourage adherence to small family norms. Unlike in developed countries where family planning is not an issue of discussion because most people practice it, in Africa, this takes a more complex dimension. Communal decisions affect all members and an individual is part of a large family, both living and dead. This is why the governments need to use methods which will make their people understand the consequences both now and in the future. The role of opinion leaders cannot be emphasized enough. These leaders play a great role in communal decision making. If there is to be any effect in family planning methods, then the opinion leaders need to be educated on the importance of family control so that they can educate the community.

There are a number of other facilities which Africa and other countries can use to start the development process. This includes expansion of educational facilities and development of the mass media to reduce illiteracy. I have noted earlier that Africa is facing a great level of illiteracy especially among those in the rural areas where the majority live. It is through education that the population can abandon traditionally held beliefs to modern beliefs and attitudes. This will make it possible for the government to acquaint the public with national goals and create a sense of nationhood.

Sociocultural Change

As far as social changes are concerned, the governments have a major role of educating their population on several issues. For example, there is a need to promote and enhance the position of women in society and make them equal partners in the development process. Liberation movements have been ongoing in many developed countries. The less developed countries should not underestimate such movements but should enhance the development of women who are the root of society anywhere in the world. Equality for all means development for all and participation for all.

The lifestyle of the people needs to be addressed. Most developing countries are changing fast. Most of these countries have cities which are identical to those in Europe and U.S. The lifestyle of the people has changed to fit developed countries models. This has made life difficult as people try to imitate a lifestyle that is too expensive to maintain. Governments in Africa have role to convince the people of the need to accept locally made products which may be cheaper to buy and maintain as compared to imported lifestyle.

Another major focus should be to examine the impacts of changes as a result of economic change, education change, religious change, change in government or environmental changes. For example, are there more male elite than women and what difference does this bring to the society? Who are the majority migrants in the cities and what effect has this brought to the rural areas? Does lack of rain affect people's decision to rely on agriculture? What other alternatives are possible and at what level should such options be adopted? How do people react when governments change hands, do they feel more confident or threatened? Is there an overall harmony in the society as a result of various social changes? All these questions are necessary in order to determine the direction the society is taking and what to expect in the future. The issue also helps in planning and implementation of several governments' policies.

Africa and Coalition

Together with the above strategies, let me credit Wriggins and Adler-Karlsoon in their book entitled *Reducing Global Inequalities* (1978:43-102) for developing what I consider applicable strategies for Africa and other developing countries.

1. Commodity coalitions: I have mentioned that most African countries have similar resources and produce similar commodities. This means that the countries can form international agreements and join together to control the supply and price of the resources in their hands. Countries like Uganda, Kenya and Tanzania have coffee as a key export commody. If the countries can come together and market their products at a single currency, the countries can have a bigger

voice in the   international market and policy making. African countries can learn from Organization of Petroleum Exporting Countries (OPEC). Although this body was initially formed as a means of influencing the policies of the Western nations toward the Middle East, the member countries have continued to maintain control over the price of the bulk of the world's petroleum resources. This has in turn increased their capital resources. The African countries have a great potential of forming such a body because many of the mineral resources that the developed countries require for industries are located in developing countries. Instead of having small bodies like the former East African Community (EAC), ECOWA, PTA and other small bodies, Africa needs to come together and form a body or bodies which will work for the best interest of Africa instead of Western nations which have ensured such unity of interest is never implemented. Division of interest will not help Africa but will continue to put her in depression.

2. Regional coalitions: The world is moving to a level whereby individual countries will not survive alone. Europe is uniting under the European Common Community (ECC), while Asian countries are uniting under the Pacific Asian Rim.   Other coalitions are the Association of Southern Asian Nations, The Andean Group in Latin America and the Organization of African Unity (OAU).

The goal of OAU was to resolve inter-African differences and reduce the frequency of conflicts while at the same time keeping world powers outside. The goal has seldom been achieved as has been currently demonstrated by many civil wars, and outsiders participation leading to political and economical upheavals.

Whether OAU has been effective or not, is impossible for Africa stand as an individual continent operating independently. There is a need for countries located in the same region to unite together and cooperate to promote their own regional development by establishing trade agreements which will serve their interests. Only through such coalitions can the countries have a strong potential for enhancing regional control over regional resources and markets, both locally and internationally.

3. Universal Coalition: Besides resource control and regional development policies, universal coalition of the countries bring together countries from all over the continent to form a single body. Developing countries can come together to form a body which would attempt to influence and reduce the gap between the rich and the poor. Also, the coalition could function both as consciousness raising groups to promote greater solidarity among Third World nations. Africa has

been politically divided into three groups: Arab North; the Sub-Sahara (black inhabitants); and South Africa. The region mostly referred to as poor Africa is the Sub-Sahara African. It is still the same region which is politically divided and economically handicapped. The coalition of Africa needs to bring the three areas together into ONE AFRICA, with a single interest: developing Africa and giving the continent a competitive economic edge.

4. Associations with a major world power: Since most African countries became independent in the 1960s, they have maintained a close link with major world powers. Although the goal of such associations has been to provide the developing countries with industrial equipment, technical advisors, and economic assistance, this has not been the case. Most of the associations are formed for political reasons. Each major power has tried to influence and manipulate the political structure of the African countries while at the same time has registered its interest, either directly or indirectly. No wonder the systems of governments in Africa vary from dictatorship to what is literally defined as democracy by the powers. As a result, Africa has been confused as to which system fits her environment and people. However, as noted early, an African system of democracy cannot be American, European or Asian. While the same principles apply, the application is different. An African democracy should consider the culture, social and economic situation of the people. A coalition with any world powers should only be necessary where economic gains are feasible and not tied to any restriction as has been the case in the past. I know some countries like to exclude themselves from universal decisions hoping to gain favor from the Western powers. However, a universal coalition and decision making can create new light for Africa. As Abraham Lincoln noted, "United we stand, divided we fall." Africa has been divided for a long time and unity is the only means of recovery.

Coalitions for nations in Africa and the world at large are inevitable. The world today is highly interdependent and will continue to be so. Stockwell and Laidlaw conclude:

> To ignore this fact (coalition) is to court disaster. The problem of Third World development has emerged as the most critical problem we face for several decades to come. Not just the well-being of the people in the countries is at stake; the well-being of all of us hangs in the balance, and it is very much in the best interests of all of us to exert the massive efforts that are and will be required to achieve some semblance of economic parity throughout the world (1981:327-328).

Education, Organization and Discipline

I have noted elsewhere that poverty, which means misery and degrades and stultifies the human person, is difficult to comprehend for those who have never experienced this dehumanizing element. Many people see poverty as a result of lack of natural wealth, or a lack of capital, an insufficiency of infrastructure or even laziness. However, as E. F. Schumacher, well known as the originator of the concept of Intermediate Technology for developing countries, and as Economic Advisor to the National Coal Board from 1950 to 1970 noted in his book *Small is Beautiful: A Study of Economics as if People Mattered,* "the primary causes of extreme poverty are immaterial, they lie in certain deficiencies in education, organization, and discipline "(1980:157). His principles are applicable and relevant to Africa. According to Dr. Schumacher, development does not start with goods. "It starts with people and their education, organization and discipline." This means that without giving attention to these three elements, resources remain latent and untapped potential. He notes that every country no matter how devastated, but with high levels of education, organization, and discipline, produces an 'economic miracle.' The central problem of development lies primarily not on poverty but on the three deficiencies and without alleviation from these deficiencies, development is almost impossible. Development cannot be an act of creation, it cannot be ordered, bought, or comprehensively planned. Development requires a process of evolution. "Education does not 'jump'; it is a gradual process of great subtlety. Organization does not 'jump.'; it must gradually evolve to fit changing circumstances. The same goes for discipline. All three must evolve step by step, and the foremost task of development policy must be to speed the evolution. All three must become the property not merely of a tiny minority, but of the whole society" (p.157).

Development in Africa can only be effective if there is better quality education among the leaders. Realizing this need, most advanced countries have assisted Africa by educating her people. Unfortunately, the education only fits the advocate countries' systems where it has been developed and implemented for years. When brought to Africa, it fails to take into consideration the African culture, environment and social structure. And when it fails, as has been the case in many countries, the Africans bear the blame. According to Dr. Schumacher, "if a given economic activity is introduced which depends on *special* education, *special* organization, and *special* discipline, such are in no way inherent in the recipient society, the activity will not promote healthy development but will be more likely to hinder it. It will remain a foreign body that cannot be integrated and will further exacerbate the problems of the dual economy" (p.158).

Government and development

Governments in Africa have played what is considered to be a central focus in development. Through central planning, most governments have used their central roles to dictate what is good for the society without any public participation and support. The governments' power and goals have not always benefited the people as decisions are made from the top and then passed down to the public who have less influence in such decisions and policies. The presence of 'white elephants' in Africa and many other developing countries has been as a result of governments' desires to match and keep pace with the developed world. The effect of central planning has been seen in the last three decades. Dictatorship and authoritarian rules have come in many cases as a result of a misuse of power to suit the governments rather than their people. In many countries this has led to upheaval as the majority and often the poor rise to oppose any of the governments' actions.

How Should The Governments Then Facilitate Development?

To facilitate development , the government is to provide the basic social and economic infrastructure that is necessary for modernization. The government needs to do the following:

1. Provide efficient and effective systems of transportation and communication. This will ensure there is means and access to markets for all produce and so that rural communities can also be reached and reach out to others. Development cannot be achieved if people are cut off from the rest of the world. The rural communities can participate in development if included in   decision making involving their areas. This will lead to developing with the people, not for the people. Working with the people (urban and rural) should lead to overall

development of a country.   Promoting one group leads unbalanced development, a common practice in Africa.

2. Education: Concerning   education, it is important to note that schools and training programs enhance the quality of the labor force. This is based on the fact that there can never be development without the public understanding   the importance composition of that development. Education is particularly important in the process of modernization. In fact, education has been used as a measure of both the level of development in a country and   an indicator of skill qualifications of the work force. A country with low a level of literacy can't be considered developed even though it may have many skyscrapers and foreign investments. A wise government will invest a lot of resources in educating its population as the first step in development. Countries like Kenya and Nigeria have put emphasis in this area. In Kenya, for example, education is compulsory for all communities irrespective of their ethnic backgrounds.

3. Public Utilities: This is another area which a government needs to devote   resources and attention. Public utilities and public health facilities are needed to provide energy and basic medical services both in the rural areas and in urban areas. Healthy people means increased life expectancies. This also ensures the labor force is healthy, leading to increased productivity. Other issues include good housing,   clean water supply, good disposal systems and pollution controls, all which lead to satisfaction and a healthy environment.

4. Rural projects: Over 80 percent of the developing countries' population live in the rural areas. However, due to a lack of necessary facilities to occupy the work force, there has been an increased migration to the cities and other urban areas. Rural projects need to be seen as means of controlling migration while at the same time developing   the rural areas. Employment will be created and congestion in the cities will be reduced. Rather than focusing on one sector in development, development of cities, governments need to have an overall focus in their countries based on country development. That means spending several billion dollars in the country side to build dams for irrigation, forest preservation promotion campaigns and tree planting,   training in better methods of agriculture and cultivation, appropriate medical facilities, increased school facilities, storage facilities for produce,   proper communication and ensuring there are no ethnic differences. This is development. It means poverty is becoming a thing of the past.

5. White Elephants: African countries and many other developing countries are known to have some of the finest and highly modernized cities in the world. Most of the countries have huge, spectacular

buildings, monuments and other structures that are meant to attract the attention of the world. These "white elephants," as they are commonly known, stand in isolation in the midst of shanties, slums, unemployment and miserable communities, some without hope for tomorrow. What is the use of working in the fiftieth floor in the heart of the city only to sleep in rags or on the street? Yet despite the great needs of the people in rural Africa, governments continue to spend thousands of dollars in development of cities.

It is worth mentioning that much of the important insights are missed when we focus on quantitative terms and in vast abstractions -- like Gross National Product (GNP), investments, savings, --- all which have their usefulness in the study of developed countries but have virtually no relevance to development problems. A major factor used to measure development is the use of GNP. This is utterly misleading and leads to a phenomena which is well defined as neocolonialism (Schumacher 1980:180). To meet the standard set by developed countries, which by the way are not the methods they used during their development stages, the African countries have struggled to sacrifice what they have. They have invited foreign investors to exploit their environment in hopes of getting the badly needed foreign currency. This makes those living in the rural areas to be neglected. It does not matter how many white elephants a country may have. As long as its people continue to suffer, it remains undeveloped. It is not the goods that makes a country developed, it is the people. Development can only be achieved when the poor are enabled to live a good life, when the uneducated are educated, and when the rural inhabitants consider themselves developed.

6. Property rights: A government cannot be considerate if it fails to protect the rights of properties. Most African countries neglect this aspects. Governments' ministers and administrators are accused of taking state properties and making them individual properties. As mentioned in Chapter Five, the culture of eating has promoted massive stealing from the state and from the poor. Development is impossible if individuals have no rights to control their properties. A government that does not protect individual properties, both for the rich and the poor, lacks credibility and respect from the people. Such a government is hard to trust. Without trust, development is impossible. Unlike the traditional periods when land was owned by the community, today individuals own lands and other facilities. Families lack interest in communal affairs. Individualism continues to have much impact in Africa. This shows the need to guide individual property rights to avoid conflicts in the society especially from those who want to take from the less abled (those who have no money to fight for their rights

in court). For development to be attained, African governments must respect all   properties and protection without discrimination or favoritism.

7. Non-burdensome taxes and government regulations: All governments require taxes to finance public expenditures both locally and abroad. However, each government needs to establish a system of taxation that does not oppress the poor or give much rights to the rich. A non-burdensome tax system and government regulations mean that the government ensures balanced taxation procedures. Proper regulation of taxation and other governments financial affairs necessity World Bank's favor or restrictions to a country's request for funds. The African governments should establish their own policies that make them credible at the international level. The public satisfactions in the existing systems necessities trust in the systems. Loopholes in the systems discourage investment, savings, and encourage evading of taxes.

8. Encourage savings: Governments should work out policies that encourage savings. Increased savings enable banks to lend more. This leads to more investment which in turn leads to more production. High production means increase in exports. Export gives a country more foreign currency. Low savings, means low investment, low exports, and lack of foreign currency. Governments can encourage savings by increasing interest on savings and controlling inflation. This will reduce fear that money deposited will loss value, a common occurrence in many African countries.

9. Conservative monetary policy: Monetary policy is the deliberate control of the money supply or credit in an economy. Money supply and the level of credits issued in an economy determines the level of inflation or deflation. Governments have different methods to control money supply in order to maintain an acceptable level. The objective of the monetary policy is to reduce the inflationary and deflationary gaps.

There are three methods used by governments to achieve the objective:

a) Open Market: Governments conduct open-market operations by buying and selling their securities. By purchasing or selling securities, the governments add or subtract money supply to or from the economy. Buying of securities increase money in the economy while selling of securities reduces money supply.

b) Reserve requirements: Governments through the Central Banks require local banks to keep a minimum percentage of deposits to back liabilities. A reduction in reserve requirements means that excess reserves can be freed up. As a result, banks are able to increase loans that lead to increased money supply. Increased in reserve requirements indicate that the banks have to reduce their loans lending capability. This way, money supply in the economy is controlled according.

c) Discount rates: This is a method used by the governments, for example the Federal Reserve System (Fed) in the U.S. to control the amount of money commercial banks and other savings and credit institutions can borrow. When banks borrow from Fed or central banks (in most Africa countries), they are said to use the *discounting windows.* In the U.S.. only those institutions holding their reserve deposits with the Fed are entitled to borrow. Let me point out that banks do not have unlimited access to the discount windows. They must exhaust all reasonable alternative sources of funds in order to borrow. The banks can only use such funds for temporary purposes. Usually, banks are charged interest (discount rates) for using discount windows.   African governments should restrict their monetary policy to make their economies remain stable. It is only and only then can development be achieved.

In summary, development has to address three key areas. The gap between the rich and the poor; the educated and the uneducated, urban lifestyle and rural lifestyle require attention. The first and key problem of any development conscious government is to try to bridge the gulfs. The society's satisfaction in necessary for development to be achieved. We cannot fit people in development but development has to fit people's needs and wants, capabilities and lifestyles.

Let me conclude this chapter using Dr. Schumacher's observation on economy and survival. He notes:

Strange to say, the Sermon
on the Mount gives pretty
precise instruction on how
to construct an outlook that
could lead to an
Economics of Survival.

-How blessed are those who know that they are poor;
the kingdom of Heaven is theirs.

How blessed are the sorrowful;
they shall find consolation.

How blessed are those of a gentle spirit;
they shall have the earth for their possession.
How blessed are those who hunger and thirst to see
right prevail; they shall be satisfied;

How blessed are the peacemakers;
God shall call them his sons.

It may seem daring to connect these beatitudes with matters of technology and economics. But may it not be that we are in trouble precisely because we have failed for so long to make this connection? It is not difficult to discern what these beatitudes may mean to us today:

-We are poor, not demigods.
We have plenty to be sorrowful about, and are not
emerging into a golden age.
We need a gentle approach, a non-violent spirit, and small is beautiful.
We must concern ourselves with justice and see
right prevail.
And all this, only this, can enable us to become
peacemakers.

. . . . I have no doubt that it is possible to give a new direction to . . . development, a direction that shall lead it back to the real needs of man, and that also means: *to the actual size of man.* Man is small, and therefore, small is beautiful. To go for giantess is to go for self-destruction. And what is the cost of a reorientation? We might remind ourselves that to calculate the cost of survival is perverse. No doubt, a price has to be paid for anything worth while: to redirect technology so that it serves man instead of destroying him requires primarily an effort of the imagination and an abandonment of fear (1980:145-146, 148-149).

Does this apply to Africa? Does this offer a solution to the African crisis?

CASE STUDY 10.1

TANZANIA: LOW MARX

Economist fashions travel fast these days. Eastern Europe's craze for economic reform has spread to Africa, where even Tanzania is beginning to heed it. Students of Marxist Leninist internationalism should take note. Tanzania staked its claim to be the heartland of Africa socialism in 1967, when Julius Nyerere, the former president, triumphantly laid out the principles of ujamaa (Swahili for "familhood"). The family was not happy.

Tanzania's ujamaa, proclaimed as a purely African construct, had practical consequences all too familiar to students of eastern Europe. Western European governments particularly Nordic ones, mistaking African socialism for their own democratic variety of it gave the story an extra twist. Western donors poured about $9.5 billion into Tanzania between, 1970 and 1985. They supported, among other things, an arrogant single party bureaucracy, the persecution of anybody seeking to provide a service for profit, and collective farms whose inhabitants were coerced into residence, and which sometimes lacked water, roads and arable land.

The World Bank financed white elephants like the $15m Morogoro Shoe Factory, designed (in the traditional of Stalinist gigantism) to produce 4m pairs of shoes per year, but which never produced more than 7% of its capacity. Nobody in Tanzania, or at the World Bank, took care of small problems like marketing and design, or saw to it that the plant got appropriate supplies of power and raw materials.

As Tanzania's GNP dropped, the government ran out of money to run its own activities. More western aid came as straightforward budgetary support, flowing straight into the hands of increasingly corrupt and numerous bureaucrats. The donor nations, disillusioned with Mr. Nyarere, began pressing him to change. He conceded that "mistakes had been made" and, on his retirement (from the presidency, though not from the chairmanship of the single party) in 1985, he left the task of economic reforms to his successor, Ali Hassan Mwinyi.

President Mwinyi devalued Tanzania's currency, cut its budget and removed some curbs on foreign investment and imports. Peasants, many of whom had slipped from cash crop farming back into subsistence farming, were paid real money again (if not much of it). Imported goods, paid for by new forms of foreign aid, began to appear in the shops. Queues shortened.

But if ujamaa felt like an invention from outside, so does economic reform. The bureaucrats -- in a one party state, they are also the political elite -- are still around, and grossly underpaid; government executives may earn as little as the equivalent of $10 monthly. But the tightly regulated, centrally administered economy gives them many opportunities to supplement their salaries. Starting a business requires permission, and hence a bribe: producing anything requires a license, and hence a bribe. The government talks of selling the subsidized state corporations which drain resources and provide comfortable niches for directors. Not a single one has been sold.

Tanzania still has Africa's largest state sector. When they do cut budgets, the bureaucrats prefer to starve social program's rather than fire the 30-40% of their own number who have no real jobs; they say that laying off 100,000 people would be "inhumane". Currently reform moves with excruciating slowness. Banking reform has yet to begin at all. The building of white elephants continues, not least in deserted, waterless Dodoma, designated the country's new capital.

Once again, western aid contributes to the problem. When Poland and Hungary appealed to the IMF and World Bank for aid in 1989, they were told they would not get a penny unless they cut the budget, implemented monetary reforms, introduced a convertible currency, privatized industry. The list for Tanzania is much the same. Little of it has been done, yet the country got more than 1$ billion in aid last year (1990), supporting the state sector that it is meant to help dissolve.

When the IMF cut off loan negotiations in 1980, the Tanzanians did move faster. But outside pressure was not maintained. As elsewhere in Africa, many donors nations are reluctant to accompany their cash with conditions even, for example, to require accounting for an import support programme. The excuses border on the racist: "This is Africa, what can you expect?" said a foreign expert, to explain why those state corporations remain unsold.

Some outsiders say progress is delayed by the lack of black capitalists. Others fear that freer markets could lead to racial strife, as local Asian entrepreneurs regain their former prominence. But a faulty system, not cultural incapacity, explains why Tanzania has few indigenous capitalists. If bribery and corruption can buy education, houses and cars, ingenious Tanzanians could surely work out honest ways of getting them.

About one-third of the western aid goes to pay for hundreds of high-earning expatriates, to do jobs that Tanzanians are supposed to be incapable of. Donors (though not America's agency, USAID) bring in foreigner, and are surprised to find that Tanzanians do not maintain their projects when they are complete.

Gradual change can lead to further corruption. When private firms were authorized to buy hard currency at special rates, subsidized by foreign donors, the bureaucrats who issued the licenses demanded bribes for doing so, and pocketed part of the proceeds. Making the currency convertible would have been more effective, and cut out the rackets.

Tanzania's one party state has avoided the worst of its neighbors' human rights abuses. For that, western governments have rewarded it with aid. But that aid has enabled the oversized government to grow even larger and less competent. Ordinary Tanzanians need feel no gratitude to the foreigners whose kind intentions have made them even poorer. With less aid, their government might have been forced to take responsibility for its failures, and to rectify them or resign.

Source: *The Economist*, London. August 14th, 1991. pp. 40, 42. Used by Permission.

Questions

1. Evaluate Tanzanian socialist type of government as a model for Africa.
2. Ujamaa is the source of poverty in Tanzania. Discuss
3. Donors' attitude toward Tanzanian government has encouraged corruption and slow development of the country. Discuss.
4. According to you, how can Tanzania solve its internal problems?
5. If you are the head of IMF of World Bank, what action would you take to a country like Tanzania to ensure development is effective?
6. Do you think Tanzania is incapable of developing itself without outside help? Explain.

CASE STUDY 10. 2

AFRICAN COUNTRIES SHOWING POSITIVE
GROWTH   THROUGH   ECONOMIC   STRUCTURAL
ADJUSTMENT

MADAGASCAR: This Could Be a Decade of Economic
Expansion

The 1990s could be a decade of economic expansion in Madagascar,
provided the country continues to adhere to its program of economic
structural adjustment under the auspices of the World Bank and
International Monetary Fund. Opportunities will exist in projects
related to rehabilitation programs funded by multilateral and bilateral
assistance programs. Additional business opportunities will develop as
result of Madagascar's effort to privatize certain state-operated
enterprises, implement its new investment code, and establish free
trade zones.

In 1990, U.S. exports to Madagascar totaled $11.5 million, a 56
percent increase over 1989, but still well below the export figures of
the early 1980s. Major U.S. exports last year were soybean oil, aircraft
parts, diesel generators, dump trucks, and TV-radio transmission
apparatus. Best trade and investment prospects are in the areas of
telecommunications, clothing manufacture, and tourism-related
projects. Development of Madagascar's titanium exports offer
intriguing investment possibilities in the longer term, as do fisheries.
However, the country's delicate environment is threatened by rapid
development and unchecked population growth, and the government
will have to adopt strategies to protect its unique flora and fauna.

Madagascar registered 3.8 percent real growth in GDP in 1990,
arising partly from new foreign investments in industry, domestic
agricultural recovery (output up 5.5 percent), and above all, significant
export recovery. Inflation was down to 9 percent, from 26.8 in 1988.

In December 1989, the Malagasy government implemented a new
investment   incentive   package,   geared   towards   privatization,
liberalization, and a greater role for market forces. It protects foreign
investors from non-commercial risks, and American investors can
obtain insurance coverage from the U.S. Overseas Private Investment
Corporation (OPIC). OPIC plans to sponsor a U.S. investment mission
to Madagascar in September.

Under the new investment law, small-and-medium-sized
companies will benefit from:

- a tax holiday of 100 percent for the first five years, declining progressively to 20 percent after 10 years;
- 100 percent exemption from import duty and value-added tax for plant and equipment setup of new ventures;
- 100 percent exemption from registration fees for the purchase of buildings for the venture. Larger firms benefit from;
- exemption from income taxes of 100 percent for the first five years, declining to 25 percent after eight;
- up to 100 percent exemption of import and value-added taxes on initial assets imported in the first three months;
- percent reduction in 'contribution duties;
- exemption from registration fees.

The Malagasy government also passed an act providing for the creation of Export Processing Zones (EPZs). The Export Processing Law applies to industrial investments in export production in three domains: industrial processing firms whose entire output is exported; construction firms concerned with equipping and promoting the free trade zone itself; and service industries which serve the two above. The law encourages establishment in three areas. Antananarivo, Toamasina, and Antsiranama, but permits an EPZ firm to set up anywhere while still enjoying the same tax advantages. Foreign investors, mainly from Mauritius, France, and Asian countries, have already invested in the export processing zones. The Far East Group, a Hong Kong-based firm, will establish, construct, and operate a free trade zone at a site near the port of Tamatave. The Far East Group has contacted U.S. Ambassador Walker, and requested assistance in identifying U.S. firms interested in constructing and operating an independent satellite telecommunications system for the Tamatave Free Trade Zone.

GABON: Rich Resource Based Makes This A Good Long-Term Market

Gabon, with its small population and substantial oil reserves, has long been one of Sub-Saharan Africa's richest countries. Per capita GNP in 1989 was approximately $3,300, putting Gabon roughly on a par with Portugal. Increased production from the newly developed Rabi-Kounga oil field has given an important boost to Gabon's economy. Gabon's GNP increased by an impressive 13 percent in 1990.

Export prospects for Gabon remain most favorable in the dominant petroleum sector. Various types of drilling equipment -- including boring and sinking machinery, casing for oil and gas drills, parts for derricks, pit-head winding gear, and line pipe for oil-accounted for the lion's share of U.S. exports to Gabon in 1990. Total American sales of oil-related items topped $26 million   in 1990. Exploration and production should see continued expansion throughout 1991, creating new possibilities for equipment sales.

Gabon also represents a significant market for other goods. For example, Gabon must meet a major part of its food requirements through imports, and the country spent more than $100 million on food purchases in 1990 alone. Thus far, U.S. exporters have been slow to penetrate this market, but U.S. food exports are growing. Sales of American wheat to Gabon nearly doubled in 1990 to over $1 million. Gabon also imports hundreds of millions of dollars worth of consumer goods, chemical products, paper productions, metals, plastics, and machinery. Aggressive American firms willing to establish Long-Term contacts through French-speaking representatives are most likely to capture a share of the market for these items.

Gabon offers a reasonably good Long-Term potential to U.S. exporters not only because of its oil wealth but also because of its mineral and forestry resources.

Government commitment to large-scale agricultural development and road construction programs should also create additional opportunities for U.S. exporters. Of special interest to exporters is the International Trade Fair of Libreville, held in March/April every year.

TOGO: Reputation is Growing As Good Place to Do Business.

Togo is a small agricultural country on the coast of West Africa that plays an important role in regional trade. Togo's capital, Lome, is home to more than 400 regional trading companies. These companies re-export to the Sahelian nations of Mali, Niger, and Burkina Faso, to neighboring Ghana, Benin, and Nigeria, and to buyers in Central African nation of Gabon, Cameroon, the Congo, and Zaire. With a modern, efficient port said to be the best in West Africa, an extensive network of paved roads to the Sahelian countries and to its western and eastern neighbors, state-of-the-art telecommunications and banking facilities, and modern hotels, Togo has gained a reputation as a good place to do business.

Togo's economic outlook for the 1990s will depend heavily on several factors: the availability of foreign donor financing, world prices for the country's four principal products -- coffee, cocoa, cotton, and phosphates -- which account for 44 percent of GDP, and the success of the country's foreign investments liberalization policies, privatization, and the recently established Export Processing Zone (EPZ).

The Togolese government's top priority is encouraging foreign investment. Togo was selected as a preferred site for an EPZ under a join effort by the U.S. Overseas Private Investment Corporation (OPIC) and the Agency for International Development (AID). Togo's selection was influenced by the availability of a willing and trainable work force, good transportation and telecommunications infrastructures, good banking facilities, a favorable investment climate, and preferential access to the European Community. The EPZ is located adjacent to the Port of Lome.

In 1989, Togo approved new investment code as well as the EPZ law. Togo's EPZ law offer generous advantages to foreign investors, including: no restriction on foreign ownership: a 100 percent, 10-year business tax holiday; complete tariff exemptions on imports and exports, including all manufacturing machinery and raw materials: rights to foreign currency accounts, the right to freely hire and fire employees; reduced payroll taxes; reduced electricity and water rates; and the right to establish private telecommunications links. To qualify, firms must be engaged in manufacturing of non-hazardous products destined 80 percent or more for the export market, or in provision of services for business already in the zone.

U.S. firms wishing to enter the Togolese market should be prepared to make personal visits and have available promotional materials in French. Given Togo's low income level, price is a very important factor in marketing products. There is demand for used items, seconds, remnants, and inexpensive manufactured goods. Togo is the used clothing and textile remnant capital of West Africa. More than 100 firms are active in this business. In 1990 the leading U.S. exports to Togo were; wheat, used clothing, dump trucks for off-highway use, polyvinyl chloride, aircraft parts, and mechanical front-end shovel loaders.

NIGERIA: Five Years of Reform Efforts Begin Showing Some Results.

Nigeria's economy is beginning to show positive results from the nearly five years of reform efforts under the Structural Adjustment Program (SAP). The government has worked to strengthen and diversify the economy through the introduction of free market policies, reduced fiscal imbalances, and promotion of growth in the agricultural and manufacturing sectors. With these efforts Nigeria has gained international support for its economic reform program.

As the same time, Nigeria's military government is preparing for a peaceful conversion to civilian democratic rule in 1992*. Key elements of the SAP are privatization or commercialization of many parastatals, the reliance on market forces to set the value of the naira, and a liberalization of the investment laws.

In 1990 the Nigerian economy expanded by 2 percent. Agriculture contributed just over 30 percent of GDP. Over two-thirds of the labor force is employed in agriculture, many engaged in subsistence, rain-fed, low technology farming. Other, more modern sectors of the economy include services, manufacturing, and government.

The petroleum sector, which provides Nigeria with about 90 percent of its foreign exchange earnings and 80 percent of government revenues, has little direct spillover into the rest of the economy, although it earns the capital to develop other sectors.

Nigeria was the second leading supplier of crude petroleum to the United States in 1990 after Saudi Arabia, with sales of $5.7 billion. Purchases from Nigeria accounted for more than 13 percent of U.S. oil imports. The stability of the country's general economic situation is highly dependent upon the international oil market.

The U.S. and Foreign Commercial Service (US & FCS) in Lagos maintains an active trade promotion program. Among the events scheduled for 1991 are a U.S. Medical Equipment and Supplies Exhibition/Seminar (Med Future '91) and a U.S. Computer, Telecommunications and Office Equipment/Seminar (CTO '91)...

There are a number of promising areas for U.S. trade with Nigeria. Best prospects identified by US & FCS include: agricultural machinery and equipment food processing and packaging equipment, telecommunication equipment, air-conditioning and refrigeration equipment, medical equipment, laboratory and scientific instruments, computers and peripheral, aircraft and parts, avionics and ground support equipment, printing and graphic arts equipment, architectural/contractor/engineering services, and cosmetic and toiletries.

GHANA: Seven Years of Reform Bring the Economy Back, But Some Obstacles Remain

Ghana's economy has made impressive strides after seven years of a stringent structural adjustment effort, known as the Economic Recovery Program (ERP). It was launched in 1983 after an extended period of economic decline and infrastructure deterioration. The response to reforms and realignment of incentives has been encouraging:

GDP growth averaged over 5.5 percent per year from 1983-89. In 1990, GDP growth fell to 2.7 percent and inflation accelerated, partly because of a poor crop due to insufficient rains.

Over the long term, steady progress in improving education, the civil service, the banking system, and infrastructure will lay a solid foundation for growth. However, the country still faces formidable structural and financial constraints. The economy remains highly dependent on foreign aid inflows. Sustainable growth will require much higher levels of domestic savings and investment. Inflation has risen steadily since August 1989, and the economy is vulnerable to fluctuations in the price of cocoa, the major export, and oil, the major import. The foreign debt, most of it owed to the IMF and the World Bank, is large relative to gross domestic product. Debt service ratios are high, though they are declining from a 1988 peak. Public sector restructuring and lack of new job opportunities add to urban unemployment, exacerbate low real incomes, and suppress consumer demand. Aid flows of $570 million in 1990, continuing through 1991, will help to support GDP growth.

The United States-owned Valta Aluminum Company (VALCO) aluminum smelter keeps the United States among Ghana's principal trading partners. Many of its inputs come from the United States. In 1990, U.S. exports to Ghana increased 15.5 percent, while imports from Ghana rose 32.7 percent from 1989 levels.

The United Kingdom is the largest supplier to Ghana because of long-standing trade links and investments, supplemented by export credit lines and aid tie-ins. Other Europeans Community members, principally Germany and France, are increasingly their market shares; exports are often tied to aid programs.

Japanese exports, mostly aid-tied, are rising rapidly. EC members and the United States are the main supplier of machinery and equipment, commercial vehicles, industrial inputs, processed food/beverages, and consumer goods, while Japan and South Korea dominate autos, utility vehicles, and consumer electronics.

Import restrictions and foreign exchange controls have been virtually eliminated. An Import Declaration Form (IDF) is required of all importers, stating that transactions must be conducted within Ghanaian law. Importers must also present Tax Clearance Certificate before clearing their goods.

Security at the ports has improved, but there may be handling and customs delays or pilferage. A handful of items are prohibited or restricted by high import excise taxes (beer/stout, cigarettes, cement pipes, roofing sheets, and asbestos/fibers). Preshipment inspection by SGS (Societe Generale de Surveillance) is required for consignments valued at over $5,000 (f.o.b.).

Opportunities in U.S. exporters of goods and services exist among projects financed by foreign donors, especially the World Bank, African Development Bank (AFDB), UN bodies, OPEC, and Arab donors. Many projects require engineering and consulting services, or specialized equipment, U.S. firms have won tenders for projects in timber sector rehabilitation, power grid extension, and road building. Ghana has initiated a campaign to refurbish Accra and upgrade the international airport.**

*The predicted date of peaceful conversion had
not taken place by the time this book was published.
**The above cases have been edited to facilitate academic purposes.
Source: *Business America.* "Africa, the Near East & South Asia." April 22, 1991. pp. 15-18. Used by permission.

Questions

1. What are the advantages of privatization? Are there some limits?
2. What are some of the strategies that the government can adopt to promote development in Madagascar?
3. Describe the Export Processing Zones (EPZs) Law as it apply to Madagascar.
4. What is the effect of having no restriction on foreign ownership?
5. Is Gabon's development in line with African development or is it foreign controlled development?
6. Evaluate Togo's foreign investment policy. How will this policy facilitate development in the country?
7. Evaluate the statement "Togo is the used clothing and textile remnant capital of West Africa." How will promoting foreign investment raise the living standard of the Togolese?
8. How does Nigerian's approach to development defer from that of Togo?
9. What advantages does Ghana get from foreign investment in the country?
10. Is increasing savings and domestic savings a solution to Ghanaian growth problem?
11. What opportunities do foreigners have in Ghana's expanding market?
12. What recommendations could you give to the African countries in relation to foreign and domestic investments?

Endnotes and Other References

Chapter Two:

A Model of "Original Sin": Rise of the West and Lag of the Rest[1] Source: *America Economic Review* (AER) Vol. 82. No.2. May, 1992. pp. 162-167.

Bailey, Ronald W. Africa, the Slave Trade and the Rise of Industrial capitalism in Europe and the United States. American History: A Bibliographic Review, 1986. 2. 1-91.

Child, Josiah. A New Discourse of Trade, 4th Ed. London: J.Hudges, not dated.

Dalby, Thomas. A Historical Account of the Rise and Growth of the West India Colonies. New York: Arno, 1972 (Originally published in London in 1690).

Darity, William, Jr. (1982a) A General Equilibrium Model of the Eighteenth Century Atlantic Slave Trade: A least-Likely Test for the Caribbean School. Research in Economic History, 1982. 7. 287-326.

_____.(1982b) " Mercantilism. Slavery and the Industrial Revolution." Research in Political Economy, 1982. 5. 1-21.

_____."British Industry and the West Indies Plantations." Social Science History. Spring 1990, 14. 117-49.

Engerman, Stanley L. "The Slave Trade and British Capital Formation in the Eighteenth Century: A Comment on the Williams Thesis," Business History Review. Winter 1972, 46, 430-43.

Findlay, Ronald, "The "Triangular Trade" and the Atlantic Economy of the Eighteenth Century: A Simple General-Equilibrium Model." Essay in International Finance No. 177. Prince ton University. March 1990.

Foster, Herbert. "Partners of Captives in Commerce: The Role of Africans in the Slave Trade. Journal of Black Studies, June 1976. 6. 421-33.

Hinschman, Albert O. The Strategy of Economic Development. New Haven: Yale University Press, 1958.

Unikori, Joseph E. "The Import of Firearms into West Africa 1750-1807: A Quantitative Analysis, "Journal of African History, 1977. 18 (3), 339-68.

_____. "Introduction" In Joseph Inikoris, ed. Forced Migration: The Impact of the Export Slave Trade on African Societies. New York: African Publishing Company, 1982, 13-60.

_____. "The Chaining of a Continent: Export Demand for Captives and the History of Africa South of the Sahara, 1450-1870." unpublished manuscript prepared for UNESCO, October 1986.

_____. "Slavery and the Revolution in Cotton Textile Production in England." Social Science History. Winter 1989. 13. 343-79.

Kea, R. A. "Firearms and Warfare on the Gold and Slave Coasts from the Sixteenth to the Nineteenth Centuries." Journal of African History. 1971. 12 (2). 185-213.

Keynes, John Maynard. The General Theory of Employment. Interest and Money. London: Macmillan, 1936.

Mars, Karl. Capital. Vol. 1. New York: Vintage. 1977 (originally published in 1869).

Metcalf, George. "A Microcosm of Why Africans Sold Slaves: Akan Consumption Patterns in the 177s." Journal of African History, 1987. 28 (3), 377-94.

Mintz, Sidney. Sweetness and Power: The Place of Sugar in Modern History. New York: Elisabeth Sifton (Viking), 1985.

O'Brien. Patrick k. "European Economic Development: The Contribution of the Periphery." Economic History Review, February 1982, 35, 1-18.

O'Brien, Patrick K. and Engerman, Stanley L. "Exports and the Growth of the British Economy From the Glorious Revolution to the Peace of Amiens," In Barbara L. Solow. ed. Slavery and the Rise of the Atlantic System. Cambridge: Cambridge: University Press, 1991: pp. 177-209.

Ricardo, David, On the Principles of Political Economy and Taxation. Cambridge: Cambridge University Press, 1951 (originally published in 1817).

Richards, W. A. "The Import of Firearms into West Africa in the Eighteenth Century." Journal of African History. 1980. 21 (1), 43-59.

Rudney, Walter. How Europe Underdeveloped Africa. London: Bogle-L'Ouverture, 1972.

Sheridan, Richard. Sugar and Slavery: An Economic History of the West Indies 1623 -1775. Baltimore: Johns Hopkins University Press, 1973.

Solow, Barbara. "Caribbean Slavery and British Growth: The Eric Williams Hypothesis." Journal of Development Economics. January-February 1985. 17. 99-115.

Williams, Eric. Capitalism and Slavery. New York: Capricorn, 1966 (originally published in 1944).

Williams, Wilson E. "African and the Rise of Capitalism" MA.Thesis, Department of Economics. Howard University, 1938.

THE MASTER FARMERS' SCHEME IN NYASALAND, 1950-1962: A STUDY OF A FAILED ATTEMPT TO CREATE A "YEOMAN" CLASS

Endnotes:

1. Colonial Secretary to Governor, Nyasaland, 12-03-46, National Archives of Malawi (hereafter NAM), MP 10802. This circular, like many similar ones, was a general one sent to other governors in the tropics. Governor, Nyasaland, telegram to Colonial Secretary, 11-10-46, NAM, MP 1,0000; for the response of the Department of Agriculture, see Director of Agriculture to Chief Secretary (hereafter C.S) 11 February 1946, MP 1000. For an excellent examination of the postwar Labor Government's approach to the question of food supply see Michael Cowen, "The British State and Agrarian Accumulation in Kenya' in M. Fransman (ed), Industry and Accumulation in Africa (Heinemann London, 1982), pp. 142-156; P. S. Gupta, Imperialism and the British Labor Movement 1914-64, (Macmillan, London 1975), especially chapter 10. See also: R. Pearce, Turning Point in Africa: British Colonial Policy, 1938-1941 Frank Class, (London 1986), pp. 188-195; and the collection of essays in R, Rotberg (ed.), Imperialism, Colonialism and Hunger: East and Central Africa (Lexington Books, Lexington 1983). A discussion of the food situation in the immediate post-war period in Nyasaland is in M. Vaughan, The Politics of Food Supply: Colonial Malawi in the 1940s' in Malawi: an Alternative Pattern of Development, University of Edinburgh Centre of African Studies Proceedings No. 25, 1984.

2. F. Cooper, On the African Waterfront: Urban Disorder and the Transformation of Work in Colonial Mombasa (Yale University Press, New haven 1987), especially the first and last chapters.

3. G. Kitching, Class and Economic Change in Kenya: the making on an African Petite Bourgeoisie, 1905-1970 (Yale University Press, New Haven 1980) pp. 315-374; B. Berman, Control Crisis in Colonial Kenya: the Dialectic of Domination (James Currey, London 1990), 366-371; M.Cowen, 'Community production in Kenya's Central Province' in J. Heyer, P. Roberts and g, Williams (eds), Rural Development in Tropical Africa (Macmillan, London 1981); S. N. Chipungu, The State, Technology and Peasant Differentiation in Zambia: A Case Study of the Southern Province 1930-1986 (Historical Association of

Zambia, Lusaka 1988) chap. V; W. Cowie and J. Momba, Zambia's Captured

Peasantry' in J. Barker (ed.) The Politics of agriculture in Tropical Africa (Sage, Beverely Hills 1984); J. Illife, A Modern History of Tanganyika (CUP, Cambridge 1979),p.553; E. Bowden and J.Moris, 'Social Characteristics of Progressive Buganda Farmers', East African Journal of Rural Development, II (1969) pp. 55-61.

4. Kettlewell to Provincial Agriculture Officers, 4-6-1951, NAM 16-3-5F.

5. For a detail study of this famine see M. Vaughan, The Story of an African famine: Gender and Famine in Twentieth Century Malawi (Cambridge University Press, Cambridge 1987); and for official policy see: R.W. Kettlewell, 'AgriculturalChange in Nyasaland', Stanford   University Food Research Institute Paper No. pp. 239-242; Governor's (Sir Geofrey Cobly) Circular of 18 January 1950, MP109, NAM. The government's approach to conservation is discussed in W. Beinart, 'The Nyasaland Post-War Development Plan: A Historical Examination of African education Development Strategies up to 1961 with particular reference to Primary and Secondary Sectors' in Malawi: an Alternative Pattern of Development, pp. 93-148. See also E. C. Mandala, Work and Control in a Peasant Economy: A History of the Lower Tchiri Valley in Malawi 1959-1960, (University of Wisconsin Press, Madison 1990) pp. 202-226. It must be stated at this point that a different agricultural project was started in 1954 in the lower Tchiri region but, unlike the Master Farmers' Scheme, it involved resettling people in specific areas where they were expected to follow agricultural rules. This experiment is discussed by Mandala (pp. 22-26) and, in passing, by Beinart.

6. For details of the Integrated Rural Development Programme see Graham Chipande, 'Smallholder Agriculture as a Rural Development Strategy, unpublished Ph.D. thesis, University of Glasgow, 1983, pp. 44-50.

7. Richard W. Kettlewell joined the Nyasaland Civil Service as an agricultural officer in the 1930s, served in all three provinces of the colony and by the mid 1940s was senior agricultural officer. From 1951 to 1951 to 1959 he was Director of Agriculture and between 1959 and 1961 he was Secretary for Natural Resources and Minister of Lands and Surveys.

8. Kettlewell's arguments for the scheme were presented in the Department of Agriculture Circular no. 2 of 1951 dated 13 July 1951, NAM 16-3-5F, 42 86. See also Kettlewell to Nye (Agricultural Advisor to the Colonial Secretary), 2 November 1953, NAM, 19-1-4R, 3342.

9. Department of Agriculture Circular no. 1 of 1953.

10. Department of Agriculture Circular no. 1 of 1953.

11. Department of Agriculture Circular no. 1 of 1953.

12. Department of Agriculture Circular no. 1 of 1953.

13. Department of Agriculture Circular no. 1 of 1953.

14. Department of Agriculture Circular no. 1 of 1953.

15. Department of Agriculture Circular no. 1 of 1953.

16. Provincial Commissioner (hereafter P.C.) to Director of Agriculture, 15 September 1952, NAM, 15-6-3F, 7916; P.C., Southern Province, to Director of Agriculture, 15 September 1952, Provincial Agricultural Officer (P.A.O.), North, to Director of Agriculture, 39 June 1953, NAM, 15-6-3F, 7916. See also Michael Black wood's comments in the Legislative Council on 11 November 1955, NAM, 15-6-3F, 7916.

17. P.A.O. (North) to Director of Agriculture 30 June 1953, NAM, 19-1-4R, 3342.

18. Director of Veterinary Services (Dr. D. E. Faulkner) to Director of Agriculture, 20-07-53, being a reply to the Director of Agriculture's Letter of 8 July 1953, NAM, 4/4/1, 15-6-3F, 7916.

19. J. Van Vensen, 'labor migration as a positive factor in the continuity of Tonga tribal society' in A. Southal (ed.), Social Change in Modern Africa (OUP, London 1961). This is also confirmed by recent research on ethnicity; see the collection of essays in L. Vail (ed.), The Creation on Tribalism in Southern Africa (James Currey, London 1989).

20. W. Watson, Tribal Cohesion in a Money economy (Manchester University Press, Mancherster 1958).

21. Settler farmers complained constantly about shortage and turnover of labor. See, for example, R. Palmer, 'Worker responses on Nyasaland Tea Estates, 1930-1953', Journal of African History, 27 (1986), pp. 116-121.

22. Agriculture Supervisor, Domasi, to Agriculture Officer, Zomba, 9 January 1956, NAM, 7-6-85, 16201.

23. P.O.A. (North) to director of Agriculture, 6 July 1955, NAM, 19-1-4R, 3342.

24. Agriculture Officer, Zomba, to Snr. P.A.O., Blantyre. 11 January 1957, NAM, 7-6-8F, 13227; Oral interview: Mrs. Kumakanga, Chilema, T.A. Malemia, Zomba, 23-04-89.

25. Almost all requires to the P.C. (North) and the district commissioners were from Nyasallanders occupying senior positions in the colony or in Northern Rhodesia and Tanganyika.

26. A good example of such farmers is Mr. Welton Bright Mwanza who wrote to the P.C. (North) as follow: 'I have spent a lot of money on my farm and store ...[is it] possible for the Bwana to allow me a paper saying this land is mine ... I have read that this happens in Kenya so why can it not happen here'. W.B.W. Mwanza to P.C. (N.P.) 4 September 1958, NMA, 16-3-5F, 4786.

27. Although the reaction to these measures is discussed below, it is by no means a complete treatment of the subject. Post-famine agricultural and conservation regulations affected many people in the country, and a thorough examination

of what they meant to Nyasaland societies would require an entire paper. The present study deals with only the issue only in connection with the Master Farmers Scheme.

28. P.A.O. (South) to Director of Agriculture, 7 February 1956, NAM, 19-1-4R, 3342.

29. P.A.O (Central) to Director of Agriculture, January 1956, NAM, 19-14R, 3342.

30. P.A.O (North) to Director of Agriculture, 10 January 1956, NAM, 19-14R, 3342.

31. Agriculture Officer, Dowa, to P.A.O. (Central), 7 January 1956, NAM, 19-1-4R, 3342.

32. Ag. Director of Agriculture to C.S., 15 September 1955, 19-1-4R, 3342.

33. Ibid.

34. Byron Tembo farming accounts enclosed in P.A.O. (North) to Director of Agriculture, 12 September 1955, NAM, 19-1-4R, 3342.

35. Ibid.

36. The farming accounts for 1955-56 in file no. 19-1-4R, 3342. For details of tobacco and African farming see J. McCracken, 'Share-cropping in Malawi: the visiting tenant system in the Central Province c. 1920-1968' in Malawi: an Alternative Pattern of Development pp. 35-65; diem, Planters, Peasants and the Colonial State; the impact of Native Tobacco Board in the Central Province of Malawi', Journal, Southern African Studies 9,2 (1983).

37. Ibid.

38. Agriculture Officer, Zomba to P.A.O. (South), 18 May 1957, NAM, 7-6-8F, 132F. 'Straddling' was common amongst many farmers in this category. For example, in Southern Rhodesia, Weinrich found that the most successful rural cultivators were those who had other sources of income which often was invested in farming. See A. K. H. Weinrich, African Farmers in Rhodesia (London, 1975) chapters 6 and 11.

39. Department of Agriculture Circular no. 3 of 1957 dated.

31 October 1957 and covering letter of 22 November 1957, NAM, 16-3-5F, 4286.

40. Ibid.

41. P.A.O. (South) to Director of Agriculture, 8 August 1957, NAM, 1-9-6F, 17550. The majority of the people prosecuted were not part of the Master Farmers project.

42. Ibid.; P.A.O. (North) to Director of Agriculture, 7 July 1957, NAM, 1-9-6F, 17550.

43. Ag. P.C. (North) to Director of Agriculture, 7 July 1957, NAM, 1-9-6F, 17550.

44. Dr. Banda had made this point in many of his speeches between 1958 and 1959.

45. For the state of the country in the 1958-59 period see the Report of the Nyasaland Commission of Inquiry, Cmnd. 814 (London, 1958), usually referred to as the Devlin Report; Report of the Advisory Commission of the Review of the Constitution of Rhodesia and Nyasaland, Cmnd. 1148-1151 (London, 1960), usually known as the Monckton Report.

46. The tension in the country during the period 1952-53 was related to the imposition of the Federation of the Rhodesias and Nyasaland but the new territorial agricultural and conservation measures, including bundling, contributed in no small measure to the general disquiet which culminated in the Thyolos and Ntcheu riots in 1953. As stated below, no study has been carried out on these disturbances. However, the protests are mentioned in passing in T. D. Williams, Malawi: a Politics of Despair (Cornell University Press, Ithaca 1968) pp. 163-4, 166; J.G. Pike, Malawi a Political and Economic History (Pall Mall, London 1968) pp. 129, 136, 154; B. Pachai, Malawi: History of the Nation (Long man: London 1973); R. Boeder, 'Wilfred Good and the Ana Murungu Church', Staff Seminar, Chancellor College University of Malawi, 1982; Robin Palmer, 'Working Conditions and Worker Responses ....', pp. 121-126; unattributable interviews.

47. L. Cliff, 'Nationalism and the Reaction to Enforced Agricultural Change in Tanganyika during the Colonial Period' in L. Cliff and J. S. Soul (eds), Socialism in Tanzania (University of Wisconsin Press, Madison 1990), Chapters 6 and 7. For a general review of literature on rural protest see A. Isaacman, 'Peasants and Rural Social Protest in Africa', African Studies Review, 33, 2 (1990), pp. 1-120.

48. Chipungu refers to those in this category as 'middle peasants.'

49. Chipungu, The State, Technology and Peasant Differentiation, chapter V; Cowie and Momba, 'Zambia's Captured Peasantry', pp. 252-264; A. Kanduza, 'Land and Peasant Politics in Chipata District, 1890s-1980', unpublished paper.

50. Unattributable interviews; Dr. Joey Power of Ryerson Polytechnic in Toronto, Canada, has recently carried our a major study on the emergence of African businessmen in southern Nyasalans, and it is clear from my long discussions with her that many Congress officials were also budding entrepreneurs.

51. Unattributable interview. African opposition to the Federation is told numerous publications including: H. K. Banda and Harry Nkumbula, Federation in Central Africa (London, 1951): R.I. Rotberg, The Rise of Nationalism in Central Africa (Harvard University Press, Harvard 1966); R. Gray, Two Nations (OUP, London 1960); Pike, Malawi; Pachai, Malawi.

52. Personal Communication from Joey Power. I am currently working on the evolution of coo-perative societies in Nyasaland, and it is evident that many leaders in the coo-operative movement were also prominent Congress members.

53. P.A.O (South) to Director of Agriculture, December 1959, NAM, 1-9-6F, 17550.
54. Snr. Agriculture Research (H. B. Ambrose) to Director of Agriculture, December 1959, NAM, 1-9-6F, 17550.

Chapter Three:

THE WHITE MAN'S BURDEN
Source: *The Economist.* "International" September 25, 1993. pp. 49-50.

Chapter Four:

What Can Africa Learn From Japan? A Look at Japan's Rise as an Economic Power and the Collaborative Relationship Between Japanese Business, Government, and Society.
Source: Khambata, Dara and Riad Ajami. *International Business: Theory and Practice.* New York: Macmillan Publishing Company, 1992. pp. 302-305.

Chapter Five:

DEVELOPING AFRICA

Endnotes:
1. This review article is based upon the following recent publications: The Anti-politics Machine: 'Development,' depoliticization and bureaucratic power in Lesotho, by James Ferguson. Cambridge University Press, Cambridge, 1990, xvi+320pp. 40.00 pound hardback. ISBN 0521 373874; Development in Practice: Paved with good intentions, by Doug Porter, Bryant Allen and Gaye Thompson. Routledge, London and New York, 1991, xxiv+247pp. 45.00 pound hardback ISBN 0415035643.
2. OECD, Development Cooperation Report, p. 14. (Paris, OECD, 1990.
3. See for instance B. S. Cohen, An Anthropologist among the Historians and other Essays. (Delhi, Oxford University Press, 1987).
4. See for instance L. Vail (ed), The Creation of Tribalism in Southern Africa (London, James Currey, 1989).
5. A. Ashforth, The Politics of Official Discourse in Twentieth Century South Africa (Oxford, Clarendon Press, 1990).
6. Ferguson is not the first author to utilize Foucault in the analysis of development. See for instance A. Escobar, 'Discourse and Power in Development: Michael Foucault and the relevance of his work to the 'Third World.' Alternatives 10 (1985), 377-400.

7. This was reviewed by Walter Elkan in African Affairs no. 366, January 1993.

8. On 'Good Government' see the special edition of the IDS Bulletin vol. 24 no. 1, January 1993. Also, R. L. Stirrat. 'Selling the Market,' in R. Dilley (ed), Contesting Markets (Edinburgh, Edinburgh University Press, 1992).

9. For an example of an author writing uncritical from within the 'development discourse, see R. Klitgaard, Tropical Gangsters (London, I. B. Taurus, 1990).

Chapter Seven

TWO MILLION VILLAGES
Source: Schumacher, E. F. *Small is Beautiful: A Study of Economics as if People Mattered.* London: Blond & Briggs Ltd., 1980. pp. 178-192

Chapter Ten

TANZANIA: LOW MARX
Source: *The Economist.* "International" August 14th, 1991. pp. 40, 42.

AFRICAN COUNTRIES SHOWING POSITIVE
GROWTH THROUGH ECONOMIC STRUCTURAL ADJUSTMENT
Source: *Business America.* "Africa, the Near East & South Asia." April 22, 1991. pp. 15-18.
Source: *Business America.* "Business Outlook Abroad: Current Reports From The Foreign Service." October 7, 1991.

Contributors:
Watkins, Chandra D. MADAGASCAR: This Could Be a Decade Of Economic Expansion.
Hawkins, Jeff. GABON: Rich Resource Based Makes This A Good Long-Term Market.
Biddle, Reginald F. TOGO: Reputation is Growing As Good Place to Do Business.
Biddle, Reginald F. NIGERIA: Five Years of Reform Efforts Begin Showing Some Results.
U.S. Embassy in Accra. GHANA: Seven Years of Reform Bring the Economy Back, But Some Obstacles Remain

BIBLIOGRAPHY

Associated Press. "ANC Land Giveaway Plan: Blacks Would Get A Third of Farmland in South Africa". Johannesburg, South Africa, January 15, 1994.

Baver, P. T. *Dissent of Development.* Cambridge, Massachusetts: Harvard University Press, 1976.

Benes, Edward. *Democracy: Today and Tomorrow.* New York: The Macmillan Company, 1939.

Bini, Obi. "OAU Holds Conference.' *Guardian.* May 28, 1980. p. 15.

Binns, J. A. "The Resources of Rural Africa: A geographical Perspective." *African Affairs: The Journal of the Royal African Society.* (Oxford University Press). Volume 83, No. 330.

Birkland, Dave. "I've Been Waiting ... My Whole Life." (in *Seattle Times*). May 11, 1994.

Brett, E. *Colonialism and Underdevelopment in East Africa.* New York: NOK Publisher, 1973.

Brown, Lester. *The State of the World 1992: A Worldwatch institute Report on Progress Toward A Sustainable Society.* New York: W.W. Norton & Company, 1992.

Lewis, James P. *Project Planning Scheduling & Control: A Hands-On Guide to Bringing Projects In On Time and On Budget.* Chicago, Illinois, Probus Publishing Company, 1991.

"Britain Makes Third World Aid Conditional." *Daily Dispatch*. June 27, 1991.

Brown, Lester R. ; William U. Chandler; Christopher F. Lawin; Cynthia Pallock; Sandra Postel; Linda Starck and Edward C. Wolf. *State of the World: A World Watch Institutes Report on Progress Toward a Sustainable Society*. New York: W.W. Norton and Company, 1985.

Burkins, Glenn. Money, Religion Bring S. "African Rivals Together." *Knight-Ridder Newspapers*. Durban, South Africa, March 3, 1994.

"Business Outlook Abroad: Current Reports From Foreign Service." *Business America*, October 1991. pp. 20-22.

Charles Krauthammer *Washington Post Writers Group*. "Mandela, History Lessons Keys To S. Africa Success." Washington, DC. May 9, 1994.

Corry, J. A. *Elements of Democracy Government*. New York: Oxford University Press, 1951.

Cooper, Robert G. *Winning at New Products: Accelerating the Process from Idea to Launch (2nd ed)*. New York: Addison-Wesley Publishing Company, 1993.

Dara, Khambati and Riad Ajami. *International Business: Theory and Practice*. New York: Macmillan Publishing Company, 1992.

Davidson, Joe. "Mandela, With Overtures to Business, Lays Out His Plans for South Africa." *The Wall Street Journal*. May 25, 1994. p. A13.

Darity, William Jr. "A Model of "Original Sin": Rise of the West and Lag of the Rest". *AEA Papers and Proceedings*. May 1992. pp. 162-167.

Dhada, Mustafah. "Changing Relationships With The Outside World: The Changing Global Balance: Outlook For Africa." *Africa Today*. Volume 38, No. 3. 1991. 3rd Quarter. pp. 5-9.

"Doing Business In Africa." *Black Enterprise*. August 1992. p. 62.

Downden, Richard. "Reflections on Democracy in Africa." *African Affairs: The Journal of the Royal African Society*. (Oxford University Press). Volume 92. No. 369. October 1993.

Dozier, Kimberly. "Cairo Conference Ends With Broad Consensus for Plan to Curb Growth." *The Washington Post,* September 14, 1994.

Duke, Lynne. "Expectations Rise on Eve of Election in South Africa." *Washington Post.* April 24, 1994.

Feldman, Gerald M. "Africa, the Near East & South Asia." *Business America.* April 22, 1991. pp. 15-18.

Ferguson, James. *The Anti-Politics Machine: Development, Depolitization and Bureaucratic Power in Lesotho.* Cambridge university Press, Cambridge, 1990.

Frieden, Jeffrey A. and David A. Lake. *International Political Economy: Perspective on Global Power and Wealth.* New York: St. Martin's Press, 1991

Gennet, Miller Ken. "State of The World: Is Grim." *Seattle Times,* January 16, 1994.

Gasser, William G. and David 1. Robert. "Bank Lending to Developing Countries." *Federal Reserve Bank of New York.* Quarterly Review, Autumn, 1982.

Hammer, Michael and James Champy. *Reengineering The Corporation: A Manifesto For Business Revolution.* New York: Harper Business: A Division of Harper Collins Publishers, 1993.

Harris, Nigel. *The End of The Third World: Newly Industrializing Countries and The Decline of An Ideology.* New York: Penguin Books, 1987.

Harrison, Paul. *The Greening of Africa: Breaking Through In The Battle For Land And Food: An International Institute For Environment and Development - Earthscan Study.* Washington DC.: : Penguin Books, 1987.

Hawley, Edward A.; Mustapha K. Pasha, and George W.R. Kalule. "Africa Today's Yesterday II." *Africa Today.* Vol. 26 (1979) No. 1.

Helm, June. *Group Dynamics in the Politics of Changing Societies: The Problem of 'Tribal' Politics in Africa.* in *Essays on the Problem of Tribe.* ed. Seattle: University of Washington Press For American Ethnological Society, 1968. p. 183.

Imperato, Pascal James. *Down Fall of A Dictator. Africa Report.* Volume 26. No. 4, 1991. pp. 24-27.

"International Bank For Reconstruction and Development." *World Bank and IDA Annual Report 1966-67.* Washington DC.: Government Printing Office, 1967. p.26.

Kalinga, Owen J. M. "The Master Farmers' Scheme in Nyasaland, 1950-1962: A Study of Failed Attempt To Create a 'Yeoman' Class." *African Affairs: The Journal of the Royal African Society.* (Oxford University Press). Volume 92. No. 368. July 1993.

Kindleberger, Charles P. and Bruce Herrick. *Economic Development* (3 ed.). New York: MaGraw Hill Book Company, 1977.

Kligaard, Robert. *Tropical Gangsters: A Man's Experience With Development and Decadence In Deepest Africa.* Basic Books: A Division of Harper Collins Publishers, 1990.

Knight, Gregory C. and James L. Newman. *Contemporary Africa Geography and Change.* Englewood. Cliffs. New Jersey: Pr entice-Hall, Inc., 1976.

Kolosou, Andrei. *Reappraisal of USSR Third World Policy. International Affairs* (5). 1990. p.42.

Mazrui, Ali A. "Africa: In Search of Self-Pacification." *African Affairs: The Journal of the Royal African Society.* (Oxford University Press). Volume 93, No. 370. January, 1994. pp. 39-42.

Mbaku, John Mukum. "Foreign Aid and Economic Growth in Cameroon." *Applied Economics.* 1993, 25, 1309-1314.

McCracken, John. "'Africa 30 Years On': An Assessment." *African Affairs: The Journal of the Royal African Society.* (Oxford University Press) Vol. 91 October 1992. No. 365.

Makidi, Ku-Nitma. "The OAU and The Quest For The Ever Elusive Goal of Economic Development." *Africa Today.* January 15th, 1988, 3rd and 4th Quarter. Volume 35. Nos. 3 & 4. pp. 38-48.

Meldrum, Andrew. "The Big Scorcher." *African Report.* May-June 1992. pp. 25-42.

"Mobutu Lifts 20 Year Ban on Rival Parties in Zaire." *The Sun*. April 25, 1990.

National Research Council, Board on Science and Technology for International Development, Environmental Change In the West African Sahel. Washington , DC.: National Academy Press, 1983.

Niel, Henry. "Kenya Protests U.S. Refuge For Dissident." *Washington Post*. July 10, 1990.

Nigel, Harris. *The End of The Third World: Newly Industrializing Countries and The Decline of an Ideology*. New York: Viking Penguin Inc., 1987.

Nsouli, Saleh M. *Structural Adjustment in Sub-Sahara Africa. Finance & Development*. September 1993. pp. 20-23.

OECD, "Development Cooperation Report." Paris, OECD, 1990. p.14.

Oliver, R and A. Atmore. *Africa Since 1800*. Cambridge: Cambridge University Press, 1967.

Paden, John N. and Edward W. Soga (ed). *The African Experience Volume 1 Essays*. Evanston: Northwest University Press, 1970.

Perlez, Jane. "Lusaka Journal." *New York Times*. April 17, 1990.

Press, Robert M. "Tanzania Faces Slow Growth." *Christian Science Monitor*. May 30, 1990. p.22.

Pollard, Sidney (ed.) *Wealth and Poverty: An Economic History of the Twentieth Century*. New York: Oxford University Press, 1990.

Randal, Jonathan C. "France Seen Reducing African Role." *Washington Post*. March 31, 1990.

"Reconstruction and Development. (Special Advertising section: South Africa)." *The Wall Street Journal*. Friday, May 27, 1994.

Redcliff, Michael R. *Sustainable Development*. New York: Methuen, 1987. pp. 20-71.

Rimmer, Douglas. "Africa's Economic Future." *African Affairs: The Journal of the Royal African Society.* (Oxford University Press). Volume 88 No. 351. April 1989. pp. 175-185.

Richard, Joseph. "Support Africa's Move Toward Democracy Too." *Christian Science Monitor.* June 4, 1990.

Rinding, Allan. "France Ties Aid To Democracy." *New York Times.* June 22, 1990.

Routledge, and Kegan Paul. *History of the Yoluba.* Lagos: C.M.S. Bookshops, 1937; Reprinted, London, 1966.

Ruffin, Roy J. and Paul R. Gregory. *Principles of Macroeconomics (4.ed).* Glenview, Illinois: A Division of Scott, Foresman and Company, 1988.

Russell, Walter. "What A Beautiful Mess In South Africa." *Los Angeles Times.* May 4, 1994.

Sai, Fred T. "Changing Perspectives of Population in Africa and International Responses." *African Affairs: The Journal of the Royal African Society.* (Oxford University Press) Volume 87 No. 347, April, 1988. pp. 267-276.

Schumacher, E. F. *Small is Beautiful: A Study of Economics as if People Mattered.* London: Blond & Briggs Ltd., 1980.

Scripps-Howard. U.S.. "Backs Global Polulation Control." *Washington Post,* January 12, 1994.

Seebohm, Frederic. "World Hunger." *African Affairs: The Journal of the Royal African Society.* (Oxford University Press). Volume 83, No. 330, January, 1984. pp. 3-9.

Staurianos, L.S. *Global Rift: The Third World Comes of Age.* New York: William Marrow and Company, Inc., 1981.

Stirrat R. L., "Developing Africa?" *African Affairs. The Journal of the Royal African Society* (Oxford University Press). Volume 92. No. 367, April, 1993, pp. 294 -300.

Steinberg, David. "Foreign Aid Askew." *Christian Science Monitor.* April 3, 1991.

Sweet, William. "World Debt Crisis. In World Economy Changes and Challenges." *Editorial Research Report.* Washington DC.: Published by Congressional Quarterly Inc.

Tanzania: "Low Marx." *The Economist.* August 14th, 1991. pp. 40-42.
"The White Man's Burden." The Economist. September 25th, 1993.

USDA, Economic Research Service (ERS), "World Indices of Agriculture and Food Production, 1950-83." Unpublished Printout. Washington, DC.: 1984.

Watson, Catherine. "Back To Normal." *African Report.* July August 1991. Volume 36. No. 4. pp. 13-16.

Wells, Elisa and Gordon W. Perkin. "Clinton Renews U.S.. Role In Key Population" Issues. *Seattle Times,* February 16, 1994).

Whitaker, Seymour Jinnifer. *How Can Africa Survive?* New York: Council of Foreign Relations Press, 1988.

Withhuhn, Burton O. *The Impress of Colonialism.* in Knight, Gregory C. and James L. Newman. *Contemporary Africa Geography and Change.* Englewood. Cliffs. New Jersey: Pr entice-Hall, Inc., 1976. pp. 31-32.

World Development Report 1978: The World Bank. Washington, DC. August 1978.

World Development Report 1984. World Bank. New York: Oxford University Press, 1984. (in State of the World p. 205).

World Development Report 1988. New York: Oxford University Press, 1988.

Wriggins, and Adler-Karlsoon. *Reducing Global Inequalities.* McGraw-Hill, 1978.

Index

Author Biography

Samuel Muriithi is a Lecturer in the Department of Commerce, Daystar University, Nairobi, Kenya. Born in Kenya, Sam received his education in both Kenya and United States of America. He has a Master of Business Administration (MBA) from School of Business and Economics, Seattle Pacific University, Master of Arts in Communications (MA), from Wheaton Graduate School, and a Bachelor of Arts degree in Business Administration and Management from Messiah College. His areas of concentration include African Economic Problems, Management, Economics, and Development. Sam has served as a consultant in Africa in areas of management, research, communication and development projects. He is the author of a book entitled *Are Managers Communicating?* and several research articles. With much desire to see Africa develop, Sam now focuses his attention on African crisis.